G000126672

MICROSOFT®
INTERNET
EXPLORER 5

Jill T. Freeze

in 10 Minutes

SAMS

A Division of Macmillan Computer Publishing
201 West 103rd St., Indianapolis, Indiana, 46290 USA

Sams Teach Yourself Microsoft®
Internet Explorer 5 in 10 Minutes

©1999 by Sams Publishing

International Standard Book Number: 1-672-31646-3
Library of Congress Catalog Card Number: 99-60519

Printed in the United States of America

First Printing: June 1999

01   00   99   4   3   2   1

Trademarks

All terms mentioned in this book that are known to be trademarks or service marks have been appropriately capitalized. Sams cannot attest to the accuracy of this information. Use of a term in this book should not be regarded as affecting the validity of any trademark or service mark.

Warning and Disclaimer

Every effort has been made to make this book as complete and as accurate as possible, but no warranty or fitness is implied. The information provided is on an "as is" basis. The authors and the publisher shall have neither liability or responsibility to any person or entity with respect to any loss or damages arising from the information contained in this book.

EXECUTIVE EDITOR
Mark Taber

AQUISITIONS EDITOR
Randi Roger

DEVELOPMENT EDITOR
Galen Grimes

MANAGING EDITOR
Lisa Wilson

PROJECT EDITOR
Carol L. Bowers

COPY EDITORS
Patricia Kinyon
Tonya Maddox
Gene Redding

INDEXER
Greg Pearson

PROOFREADERS
Cynthia Fields
Maryann Steinhart

TECHNICAL EDITOR
Galen Grimes

INTERIOR DESIGNER
Gary Adair

COVER DESIGNER
Aren Howell

LAYOUT TECHNICIANS
Juli Cook
Darin Crone

Contents

Introduction xi

1 Installing Internet Explorer 5   1

Getting the Goods: Where You'll Find Internet Explorer 5 1
Things to Consider Before You Install the Newest
    Version of Internet Explorer 2
Downloading Internet Explorer Over the Internet 4
Which Components Do You Really Need to Install? 5
Working Your Way Through the Setup Wizard 7
Help! Something Went Wrong During Installation!..........................11
Updating Internet Explorer 5 11

2 Customizing Your Start Page   12

Test Driving Internet Explorer 5...12
Customizing Internet Start 13
Getting a New Start in Life 18

3 Navigating Internet Explorer 5   21

Anatomy of the Internet Explorer 5 Screen 21
The Title Bar..21
It's the Size That Counts...23
What's on the Menu (Bar)? 24
Back!...25
About Face! (or Forward)...25
Stop the World (Wide Web), I Wanna Get Off! 26
Freshening Up Your Data 26
There's No Place Like Home 27
Search Me! 27
Playing Favorites Another Way 28
Revisiting the Historic Past 29
One-Stop Communications Shop 31
A Copy for Your Records? 31
Addressing Your Web Browser...31
See the Whole Picture..32

Give Me Your Status 32
There's More Than One Way to Reach a Web Site 33

4 Getting Help in Internet Explorer 5   36

Introducing AutoComplete for Forms 36
Modifying AutoComplete Forms Settings 37
Remember Me, IE...38
The Help Files..40
All Kinds of Helpful Goodies..42

5 Working with Your Favorite Web Sites   43

What Is a Favorite?...43
Should I Really Save It as a Favorite? 43
Saving a Web Site as a Favorite 44
Viewing a Favorite 46
Creating a Shortcut to a Web Site on Your Windows Desktop 47
Organizing Your Favorite Web Sites...49
Deleting a Favorites Page 51

6 Sharing Your Favorite Web Sites   52

Sharing Your Favorite Web Sites 52
Dealing with Email Sharing 57

7 Browsing Web Sites Offline   59

Why Browse Web Sites Offline? 59
Saving a Web Page as a Favorite and Making It Available Offline ..59
Making a Favorite Site Available Offline 63
Manually Synchronizing Your Offline Favorites 65
Viewing Your Favorite Pages Offline 67

8 Safe, Secure Surfing   69

Dispelling the Myths of Online Security 69
Defining Security Zones..69
Setting the Level of Security 71
Assigning a Site to a Specific Zone 72
Protecting Children from Inappropriate Content 74
Setting Up the Content Advisor 74
Disabling the Content Advisor 79
Changing Content Advisor Settings 80

9   Finding Sites Online   81

How Do I Find the Good Stuff? 81

Staying On Topic: The Value of Subject Indexes 83

The Least You Need to Know About Search Engines 85

Searching Internet Explorer Style.....................................89

Searching with the New Search Assistant 90

Express Searching: When Only the Fastest Will Do 92

Finding Things on a Web Page..93

**10   Setting Up Outlook Express to Send
       and Receive Email   95**

Getting Outlook Express Ready to Receive Email.............95

Adding an Email Server to Outlook Express 95

Migrating to Outlook Express 98

Importing Email Messages into Outlook Express 99

Changing the Sound that Plays when New Mail Comes ...100

11   Sending Email with Outlook Express   103

The Anatomy of the Outlook Express Workspace 103

Composing an Email Message 107

Attaching a File to Your Message....................................112

**12   Advanced Outlook Express Mail
       Sending Options   114**

Working with Outlook Express Stationery.......................114

Building a Signature File 116

Spell Checking Your Messages..121

13   Setting Up Your Address Book   124

Adding Information to Your Address Book 124

Automatically Add Contacts to Your Address Book 127

Composing a New Message Using Address Book Information......128

Working with the Select Recipients Dialog Box 129

Editing a Contact's Information 130

14   Reading Email   132

Assessing What You've Got 132

Reading a Message 134

Reading File Attachments...135
Taking Action on a Message...137
Checking for New Messages 142

15   Setting Up Outlook Express to Be Your Newsreader   144

Add a News Server to Outlook Express...........................144
So How Do I Find the Good Stuff? 145
Subscribing to a Newsgroup..147
Unsubscribing to a Newsgroup..149

16   Posting and Reading News Articles   150

Reading a Newsgroup..150
Posting Your Own Message to a Newsgroup 154
Canceling an Article You Posted 156
Viewing Replies to Your Post 158

17   Working with Outlook Express Offline   159

Composing Email Messages Offline 159
The World of Offline Newsreading 160
Preparing Newsgroups for Offline Browsing...................161
Downloading Certain Messages 162

18   Locating a Specific Message in Outlook Express   165

Getting Your Email Organized 165
Filtering Email 167
Finding a Newsgroup Message..170

19   Outlook Express Housekeeping and Maintenance Issues   174

Avoiding the Virtual Pack Rat Syndrome.........................174
Compact Mail Folders 175
Marking Newsgroup Messages as Read and Viewing Only
    New Posts 175
Remove Old News Messages 178
Compact Stored Messages 179

20   Building Web Pages with FrontPage Express 181

Learning the Lay of the FrontPage Express Land 181
Formatting Web Page Text 182
Linking: What the Web's All About 184
Including Images on Your Web Page 188
Publishing Your Web Page 189

**21   Communicating with Others in
        Real-Time Using NetMeeting   191**

Getting to Know Microsoft NetMeeting 191
Setting Up NetMeeting 192
The NetMeeting Workspace 195
Making a Call Using NetMeeting...198
Receiving a Call 199
Participating in a NetMeeting Text Chat 200
Using the Whiteboard to Communicate Ideas 201

**22   Chatting on the Internet Using
        Microsoft Chat   203**

What's the Deal With Microsoft Chat? 203
Getting Ready to Chat with Microsoft Chat.....................................204
Understanding the Microsoft Chat Environment 209
Engaging in a Simple Chat..211
The Chat Toolbar: Your Guide to Advanced Functions
    at a Glance 212

Index   215

About the Author

Jill T. Freeze is a freelance management consultant who has worked with such organizations as the John F. Kennedy Center for the Performing Arts, the National Endowment for the Arts, The Smithsonian Institute, and the White House. Having used computers extensively over the past decade for work and play, Jill finally decided to put her experience to good use writing computer books. She authored *Peter Norton's Complete Guide to Office 2000* (Sams, 1999), *Sams Teach Yourself Internet Explorer 5 in 24 Hours* (Sams, 1999), *Sams Teach Yourself Computer Basics in 24 Hours* (Sams, 1998), *Using Microsoft Office 97* (Que, 1997), and *Introducing WebTV* (Microsoft Press, 1997). Her formal education includes a bachelor's degree magna cum laude from the University of Massachusetts at Amherst (in Arts Administration and Writing) and a master's degree from George Washington University (in Nonprofit Administration). For fun, Jill likes listening to music, writing fiction, watching NASCAR races (Go Terry Labonte!), surfing the Net, playing her flute, and playing with her two children, Christopher and Samantha. Jill can be reached at JFreeze@JustPC.com. You can also visit her Web site at www.JustPC.com.

Dedication

This one's for Veronica, Scott, Bryce, and Jesse—your family's complete at last! Much love, happiness, and health to you all!

—Jill

Acknowledgments

A special thanks to Randi Roger and Mark Taber for giving me the opportunity to produce another great book for Sams. I'll bet you didn't think I could do it in a week!

And to the terrific editing team who pulled everything together: Galen Grimes, Carol Bowers, Pat Kinyon, and Tina Perry. I can't thank you all enough for your help, speed, thoroughness, and sense of humor!

I also owe a great deal of gratitude to my husband, Wayne, and my mom for nursing me through nasty oral surgery as I wrote this. Thanks for putting up with my crankiness!

To my sweet children, Christopher and Samantha, you two are the most precious little beings on Earth. I love you with all my heart.

I'm sure there are tons of other behind-the-scenes people who deserve special recognition here, but I haven't met them yet. But even if I never do learn their names in time for them to be committed to print, please know that your hard work is much appreciated.

Tell Us What You Think!

As the reader of this book, you are our most important critic and commentator. We value your opinion and want to know what we're doing right, what we could do better, what areas you'd like to see us publish in, and any other words of wisdom you're willing to pass our way.

You can fax, email, or write me directly to let me know what you did or didn't like about this book—as well as what we can do to make our books stronger.

Please note that I cannot help you with technical problems related to the topic of this book, and that due to the high volume of mail I receive, I might not be able to reply to every message.

When you write, please be sure to include this book's title and author as well as your name and phone or fax number. I will carefully review your comments and share them with the author and editors who worked on the book.

Fax: 317-581-4770

Email: office_sams@mcp.com

Mail: Mark Taber
         Associate Publisher
         Sams Publishing
         201 West 103rd Street
         Indianapolis, IN 46290 USA

Introduction

The hardest part of writing any book is coming up with a captivating introduction—one that draws the reader in without sounding like a bunch of marketing hype. After writing six books, I still haven't got the hang of it. But one thing's clear; if you're reading this book, chances are you're a busy person who wants to learn as much as you can in as little time as possible. That lets me off the hook with all the fancy stuff and lets us get right down to business!

Internet Explorer 5 is Microsoft's latest version of its popular Web browser, but it's much more than that. It's a suite of applications designed to work together to help you do just about anything over the Internet. Whether you want to chat, send email, build your own Web page, or brainstorm on an idea with colleagues across the globe, Internet Explorer gives you the tools to do it.

Who Should Read This Book?

This book is the one for you if you can answer "yes" to any of the following:

Are you new to the Internet and just starting to learn about Web browsers and the various things you can do on the Internet?

Do you want a small volume to sit on your desk that you can consult whenever you need to?

Do you want to learn how to exploit Internet Explorer 5's newest features to enhance your personal productivity?

Do you prefer books that break tasks up into small, manageable chunks so they're easier to learn?

Are you looking for a fast, no frills, the-least-you-need-to-know approach to learning this suite of applications?

Are you tired of large, overpriced computer books that spend too much time on background material and too little time teaching you how to do something useful?

Yes? Well read on, and thank you for joining us!

How to Use This Book

For your convenience, this book is divided into 10-minute long lessons that help you learn about a specific Internet Explorer function or tool. While we realize that not everyone may be able to complete the lessons in that short a time, it's our goal to break subjects down in such a way that you can quickly and easily learn them without a huge time commitment. Such a structure also makes finding what you need a whole lot easier!

Since Microsoft is always issuing bug fixes or interim updates to its software, you may encounter subtle differences between what you see in this book and what you see on your PC. Don't be alarmed. If Microsoft does issue updated software and the steps you need to take aren't obvious, then visit my Web page at www.JustPC.com and follow the links to this book. I'll try to post answers to commonly asked questions and such so that you'll never be left in the dark.

Likewise, if you notice something that should be changed or updated in the text or you simply have a question that's not covered within these pages, feel free to send me email at JFreeze@JustPC.com. I eventually answer every piece of email I get, but it can take awhile on occasion when I'm in the middle of a book. Not meant as a deterrent, just a friendly warning <grin>!

LESSON 1

Installing Internet Explorer 5

In this lesson, you'll learn how to get hold of a copy of Internet Explorer 5 (if you don't already have it), and you'll also explore a number of installation-related issues.

Getting the Goods: Where You'll Find Internet Explorer 5

When it comes to getting your hands on Microsoft's latest and greatest Web browser and accompanying components, you'll have plenty of options. And the best part is that it may not cost you a dime!

Here are some of the ways you can expect to get the latest release of Internet Explorer:

- Get it preinstalled with a new computer purchase.

- Download it for free over the Internet from Microsoft's Web site. (This may take a fair amount of time—I'm talking two hours or more for a full install of the suite with a 56k modem.)

- Receive it as part of your Internet service provider sign-up/ welcome package.

- Buy it on CD-ROM.

- Buy a popular computer magazine and get it free on CD-ROM (though I'm told the duration of this promotion will be very short).

- Acquire it as part of a bundle of Microsoft software.

- Purchase the book *Sams Teach Yourself Internet Explorer 5 in 24 Hours* and then install the suite from the accompanying free CD-ROM.

Things to Consider Before You Install the Newest Version of Internet Explorer

While Internet Explorer 5 installation is pretty straightforward, there are definitely some things you'll want to consider and do before making the big change.

Windows 95 Users, Take Note!

If you're a Windows 95 user currently running Internet Explorer 4, you'll want to consider the following. Before Windows 98 was released, the Active Desktop technology was available for free download as a Windows update for Internet Explorer 4. Now the capability is buried within Windows 98, so it's no longer treated as part of the browser suite.

So what's the big deal? This Active Desktop-enabling Windows update cannot be imported into Internet Explorer 5. Unless you plan to get Windows 98 in the near future, you'll have to add the Windows update to Internet Explorer 4 before you overlay the newest version of Internet Explorer. Doing this enables you to keep your Active Desktop capabilities while running both Windows 95 and Internet Explorer 5.

Installing the Windows Update Under Internet Explorer 4

Follow these quick steps to install the Windows Active Desktop update:

1. On your Windows 95 **Start** menu, point to **Settings** and then click **Control Panel**.

2. Double-click **Add/Remove Programs**.

3. Select **Microsoft Internet Explorer 4.0** and then click the **Add/Remove** button.

4. Click **Add Windows Desktop Update from Web Site**. If the option does not appear, the update has already been installed on your machine.

Is There Space for Internet Explorer on My Computer?

Depending on how much of the suite you decide to install, the amount of disk space needed to house the Internet Explorer 5 files can range from 12MB to more than twice that size with all the bells and whistles.

Before you start downloading and installing the software, you may want to check the amount of space available on your system to make sure you have enough room for everything. Doing so will help you avoid the hassles of partial installation and such, not to mention frustration. In fact, if you download Internet Explorer from Microsoft's Web site, the sophisticated setup wizard will check to see if you have enough disk space on your machine; it will abort the download if you don't. You should note, however, that the wizard will want to see 90MB of free space even though it doesn't need that much.

 Give me space! There are typically two kinds of files you can safely delete to free up disk space. These include *.bak (backup files) or *.tmp (temporary files) files. In both cases, however, you should take the time to verify that either the original file is intact or that you no longer need the file.

Checking the Amount of Free Space on Your System

One way to guarantee that the setup wizard doesn't thwart your efforts is to check the available disk space in advance. To learn how much free space there is on your computer, follow these simple steps:

1. On the Windows **Start** menu, point to **Programs** and click **Windows Explorer**.

2. Look at the bottom of the program window to the right of
the status bar. The amount of free disk space will appear in
parentheses. Anything more than 50MB should be more than
enough room to proceed with the installation.

3. Click the **Close** button to exit Windows Explorer.

 Show me! If you're anything like me, you like seeing
data represented graphically. The amount of free disk
space means nothing to me, since I have little concept
of the number's relation to the total amount of disk
space on my system.

To view the amount of free disk space in a more
meaningful way, follow steps 1 and 2 above. Select
the C: drive of your machine and then open the File
menu and click **Properties**. A graphic like the one
shown here should appear, showing you exactly how
much space is available.

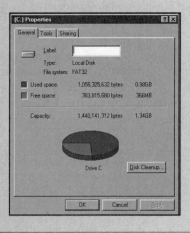

Downloading Internet Explorer Over the Internet

The fastest, most cost-effective way to get Internet Explorer 5.0 is to
download it directly from Microsoft's Web site at www.microsoft.com.

Click the **Download** link and work your way down to the **Download Internet Explorer 5** link. Click the link to begin the download.

The setup wizard will be downloaded first. The primary Internet Explorer download site can support up to 75,000 users, but even that can get filled to capacity. If it does get filled, you'll need to select an alternate download site from within the setup wizard. Never fear, though; your options will be in clear view to minimize any potential confusion.

Fast is relative I referred to downloading Internet Explorer 5 as being a "fast" way to get the new release, but I don't want you to get the wrong idea. The download could take two hours or more, though the minimal install should be completed within a half-hour or so. Of course all this depends on the speed of your Internet connection, the amount of traffic on the Net, and so forth. In this case, "fast" means downloading it will probably be the quickest way to get a copy of the product.

The first thing that will happen when you begin the download is the Internet Explorer 5 Setup Wizard will be downloaded. This should easily take five minutes or less. To run the setup wizard, click the **Start** button on the Windows taskbar, select **Run**, and then click the **Browse** button to locate the wizard on your hard drive. Click **Open, OK** to run the wizard.

Which Components Do You Really Need to Install?

While an answer of "it depends" may sound lame, there's a whole lot of truth to it. Whether you want to minimize download time or simply save disk space, you'll want to give some thought to which of Internet Explorer's components you really want and need. Let's take a closer look at each one:

- **Internet Explorer**   A Web browser and essentially the heart of the whole Internet Explorer 5 suite of applications. This item should be included in every configuration of the installation.

- **Outlook Express**   An email client and newsreader. Unless you work for a company that uses a particular messaging product, you'll need to install this element in order to send and receive email and participate in newsgroups. It should also be noted that Outlook Express gives you rich HTML message composition tools so that HTML-formatted messages can be sent and received with minimal hassle.

> **HTML**   Outlook Express' HTML capability means users can now send and receive messages that contain links to Web sites or documents on an intranet. HTML messages may also sport fancy backgrounds and fonts.

- **NetMeeting**   A tool that enables people to communicate from remote locations by audio or video (as camera availability permits). It also comes with a basic chat program, an electronic whiteboard that everyone can share, and the ability to collaborate on Office 2000 documents. Even if you don't have a professional reason to use it, if you know others who have the program, you might have some fun playing with it.

- **FrontPage Express**   A lightweight Web page design program. If you plan to design a Web page and don't want to be bothered with learning HTML, this program is for you!

- **Microsoft Chat**   An Internet chat program whose claim to fame is letting you chat with others as a comic strip character. The downside is that you need to be chatting with others using the same program in order for it to be any fun. It's not a very large program, but you may want to skip it if most of the chat rooms you frequent are powered by Web technology.

- **Microsoft Wallet** A tiny application that was created to help users conduct business safely over the Internet. It saves credit card information securely, organizes shipping addresses, and so on. Unfortunately, merchants need to support use of the Microsoft Wallet, and very few do. You may want to skip it.

The other options include such things as multimedia and foreign language support. The items you choose to install depend on your personal preferences, whether you have a sound card and speakers, and so on. Even if you don't install these items in the very beginning, they're very easy to install on-the-fly when you do need them.

Working Your Way Through the Setup Wizard

When you launch the setup wizard, the License Agreement screen shown in Figure 1.1 appears. Click the **I accept the agreement** button and then click the **Next** button:

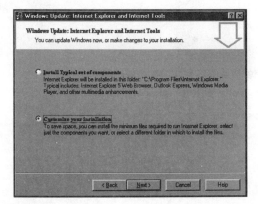

Figure 1.1   Use the scrollbars to read through the lengthy license agreement.

Once you've accepted the license agreement, you need to follow these steps in order to complete the download and installation:

1. In the Folder Destination screen (which you'll see only if you chose Minimal or Customize install), you are asked to select the location in which to install the new Internet Explorer. The default location is probably the most trouble-free. Click **Next** to continue.

2. Now for the fun part—choosing the type of installation you want. (See Table 1.1 to learn which components are included in each installation.) You can choose **Typical**, **Minimal**, or **Customize** (see Figure 1.2). Simply click the appropriate option. If you choose **Minimal** or **Customize**, you'll see a Component Options screen like the one shown in Figure 1.3. Just click the desired components and then click **Next** to move to the next step. You can also use the drop-down box to make your selection from minimal, typical, or customize installations.

Component	Minimal	Typical	Customize
Internet Explorer 5	X	X	X
Outlook Express	X	X	
Microsoft Media Player	X	X	
Other Multimedia Enhancements	X	X	
Microsoft NetMeeting	X		
Microsoft Chat 2.1	X		
FrontPage Express	X		
Web Publishing Wizard	X		
Microsoft Wallet	X		
Foreign Language Support	X		

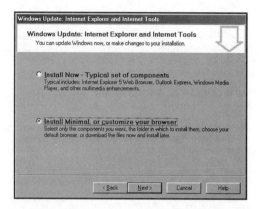

Figure 1.2

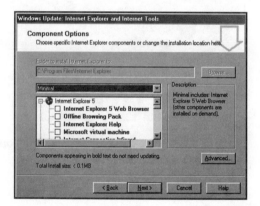

Figure 1.3 The Component Options menu lets you take what you want and leave what you don't want.

 It's not the end of the world... If you choose the Minimal install, you should know that the other components can be installed on demand at a later date.

3. The Internet Setup Wizard will let you know that it's preparing the setup—literally telling Microsoft's computer which parts you want to download. While this is going on, you may want to take the opportunity to save and exit all other applications currently running on your desktop. This is a good idea since you will need to reboot your system following the download and installation.

4. The download progress bar (see Figure 1.4) keeps you apprised of where things stand.

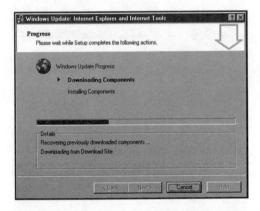

Figure 1.4 The Internet Setup Wizard will always tell you where you stand.

5. Once the chosen components have been successfully downloaded, the wizard will begin installing them on your system. Again, a progress bar will keep you informed of where you stand.

6. When the Internet Explorer 5 Setup Wizard has finished installing the desired components, you will be asked to shut down and then restart your system. This will initialize the installation.

Congratulations, you're now the proud owner of Internet Explorer 5!

Help! Something Went Wrong During Installation!

We've all been there before—working feverishly at our computer searching for that elusive piece of information on the Internet when BOOM! The link dies. That's right, all ties to the online world vanish right before your eyes. So how does that affect a major software download like the one outlined above?

Not much at all, thanks to Microsoft's new Smart Recovery tool. Should your Internet connection fizzle out midway through the download, you'll receive a series of online prompts telling you how to recover from your specific situation (see Figure 1.5). In most cases, all you'll have to do is restart the wizard. But don't worry; the entire job won't need to run from the beginning again. Smart Recovery will figure out what's already been downloaded and what hasn't and then will resume the job.

Updating Internet Explorer 5

On occasion, Microsoft will release an update to its products. Perhaps it's a bug fix or a remedy for a security leak. Whatever the case, you may want to download the patch or update from the Web to cure the problem.

When an update becomes available, the Windows Installer may prompt you to download the file. If it doesn't, you can always check the Download hyperlink on Microsoft's Web site at www.microsoft.com and then proceed from there.

In this lesson, you prepared for the installation of the Internet Explorer suite of applications. Admittedly it was much more than a 10-minute undertaking, but you know what they say about good things coming to those who wait....

In the next lesson, I'll show you how to customize your Internet Start page.

LESSON 2

Customizing Your Start Page

This lesson focuses on helping you get an Internet Start page that adequately meets your needs.

Test Driving Internet Explorer 5

Okay, let's see if it works! Establish your connection to the Internet and then launch Internet Explorer 5. (Either double-click the IE icon on your desktop or select Programs, Internet Explorer from the Start menu.) Windows 98 users can click the Internet Explorer icon on the Windows Quick Launch Bar.

The Internet Explorer 5 splash screen pops up while the browser busily grinds away in the background. Within a few moments, something referred to as the *default home page* appears. This default home page, or *Start page*, is sort of your springboard to surfing on the Net. You can use links on that page to weave your way through the World Wide Web.

When you install Internet Explorer 5, you'll see a Welcome to the Web page that asks you to supply your zip code, city, and other information. While providing this information is totally voluntary, Microsoft uses it to deliver personalized content such as local news and weather on the default Start page. The Microsoft Internet Start page appears once you've entered the requested information and clicked the onscreen Enter button (see Figure 2.1). While you can specify a different Web page to serve as your default Start page (you'll learn how to do this later in the lesson), this one will do until you become more familiar with the Internet and the Web browser itself.

Hey, that's not what I see!   If Internet Explorer 5 came preloaded on your new computer, you may be directed to an entirely different Start page. For example, my newest Gateway computer pointed me to a special Yahoo! page just for Gateway. If you don't see the Microsoft page described below, don't sweat it. You'll more than likely find plenty of onscreen prompts telling you how to customize the page they've given you.

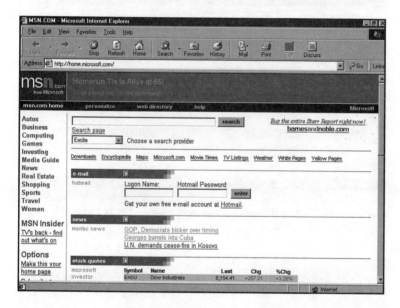

FIGURE 2.1   Microsoft's Internet Start page—where your journey begins.

Why don't you customize it to reflect things that interest you?

Customizing Internet Start

With a little bit of playing around, you'll get a home page you may actually want to read! Just follow these simple steps:

1. With the Internet Start page fully loaded, click the **Personalize** button on the black menu bar. The Personalize page, shown in Figure 2.2, appears.

Click here to begin personalizing your Start page.

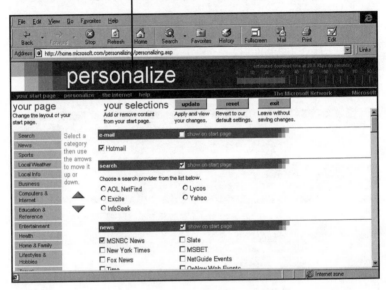

Figure 2.2 The Personalize page is the easiest way to see all of your options at once.

  But what about those arrows?   The Internet Start page also says you can click the arrows next to a category in order to customize it. While that certainly is an option, I've chosen to use the Personalize page because it enables you to see all of your choices at once and is more flexible to deal with.

2. Systematically work your way through each category to determine whether you want to keep the category at all (see Figure 2.3). If you don't want to keep it, click the check mark in the

Show on MSN.Com Start Page check box to remove it from
the page. If the category does hold some interest, select the
items within the category you want to view on startup.

Making a list and checking it twice   Remember,
simply click an item's check box to select or deselect it.
A single click will toggle the check mark's appearance.
For example, if you click a box with a check mark, the
check mark will disappear. If you click an empty check
box, the opposite will happen—a check mark will
appear.

Click here to select an item.

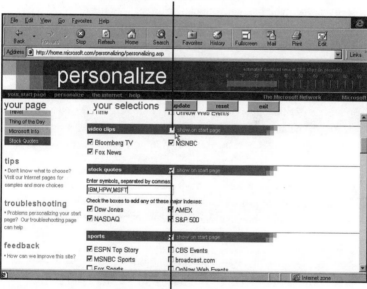

Click here to remove an item.

FIGURE 2.3   Make your selections with a single mouse click.

3. When you get to the Stock Quotes section, you are asked to
supply the symbols of the stocks you want to track, separated by
commas. Simply move your mouse pointer to the inside of the

text box provided, click once to set the insertion point, and then begin typing. It's as easy as that!

4. Microsoft also gives you the opportunity to include a sports scoreboard on your home page. In the Scoreboard part of the Sports section, you can elect to follow a single team of your choice in each category by simply clicking it. There are lots of teams, so don't forget to use those scrollbars!

 More, more, more! Don't despair, you're not limited to one team. Hold the Ctrl key down and choose as many teams as you want by clicking them!

5. Just when you thought your choices were winding down, you get to define your locale to get local weather info, enter your sun sign for your horoscope, and even include a variety of educational, family-oriented resources. The choices never seem to end! Just keep in mind that the more you include, the longer it will take your Start page to load when you launch the browser. In fact, take this opportunity to glance at the download meter at the top of the page (see Figure 2.4). If the green bar is nearing the right edge of the screen, you may want to trim your selection a bit.

6. Once all of your selections have been made, return to the top of the Personalize page. Down the left side of the screen, you'll see a series of light blue buttons labeled with the names of each category from which you chose content.

7. Click the first button to highlight it and then use the arrows to move it up or down into the desired position (see Figure 2.5). This enables you to prioritize your content.

Keep your eye on the download time meter.

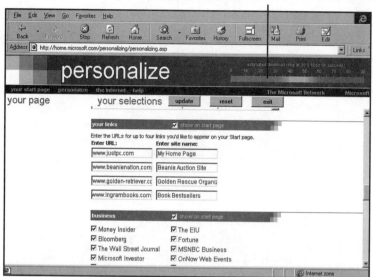

FIGURE 2.4 If you're seeing red, much download time's ahead!

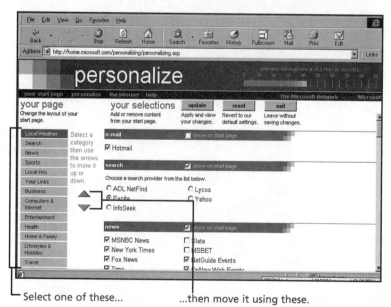

Select one of these...   ...then move it using these.

FIGURE 2.5 The Personalize page makes it easy to place the
content you want where you want it.

8. Once the topics are all placed in the order you want them, click one of the following buttons:

- **Update**   To apply and save your changes.

- **Reset**   To cancel everything and revert to Microsoft's defaults.

- **Exit**   To leave the Personalize page without saving your changes. (In other words, the Start page will stay the way you left it when you launched the browser. The adjustments you made this time will not be reflected on the page.)

Do I want Reset or Exit?   While their definitions may muddle their meanings a bit, the best way to get it straight is this: Use Exit if you're playing with a Start page you've already modified to your liking and decide to scrap your changes from this session. That keeps your previous settings intact. If you were only clowning around with Microsoft's settings to see what choices were available, either option is really fine.

9. If you selected **Update**, your newly modified Start page begins loading. This ultimately brings you back to the Internet Start page, which is now truly your Internet Start page.

Getting a New Start in Life

This section may not change the course of your life, but it can make life a bit easier (and in some cases more pleasurable).

Microsoft's Internet Start page doesn't claim to fulfill everyone's needs for a Start page. Sure, it's generated from some of the premiere sites on the Internet, but in a lot of cases that just doesn't cut it.

Have you designed your own Web page containing all of your favorite sites? Does your company's intranet have a special Web page updated with all the latest and greatest information? Is there currently a Web site dedicated to professionals in your field or to a passionate interest of yours? If so, there may be better alternatives out there for your Internet Start page. The sections that follow show you how to get the Start page you want.

Defining a New Internet Start Page

Follow these steps to configure another Web page as your default Internet Start page:

1. Make sure you have the URL of the Web site you want to define as your new default. If you can't remember the URL, launch Internet Explorer and surf over to it using your Favorites list.

2. With Internet Explorer up and running, click the **Tools** menu item and select **Internet Options**. The dialog box shown in Figure 2.6 appears.

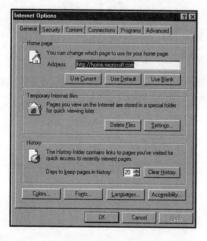

FIGURE 2.6 The Internet Options dialog box's General tab lets you define your new default Start page.

3. In the **Home Page** section of the dialog box, do one of the following:

   - Type the URL of the page you want to use in the text box provided.

   - If the desired page is currently onscreen, click the **Use Current** button.

Enough is enough! Some people like starting with a clean slate because they always go somewhere different. If this is you, you may want to click the **Use Blank** button as your preferred startup page option so that nothing is preloaded when you launch the browser. Doing this also increases the speed with which the Web browser launches and becomes fully useable; this way it doesn't need extra time to download a special page.

4. Once you've made your selection, click **OK** to apply it. The next time you launch Internet Explorer, your chosen site will be the first thing you see! (If you chose the Use Blank option, you'll draw a blank.)

LESSON 3

Navigating Internet Explorer 5

This lesson acquaints you with the Internet Explorer workspace and shows you how to get around within the Web browser.

Anatomy of the Internet Explorer 5 Screen

Using a piece of computer software without being familiar with all the buttons and menus is like driving across country without a good current map. You may be able to figure out how to do something yourself, but the path you take may not be the most efficient one.

Take a few moments to study Figure 3.1. Each major button and screen element is identified with a callout. This will give you a great frame of reference for when we discuss the elements more thoroughly later in the lesson.

The Title Bar

The dark blue strip across the top of the Internet Explorer 5.0 screen is known as the *title bar*. In the case of Internet Explorer, it holds the title of the current Web page followed by the name of the application (Microsoft Internet Explorer).

There's even more significance to the information contained in the title bar, however. When you save a Web page as a Favorite (more on this in Lesson 5, "Working with Your Favorite Web Sites"), Internet Explorer uses the page's title as the title of the item on the Favorites list (see Figure 3.2).

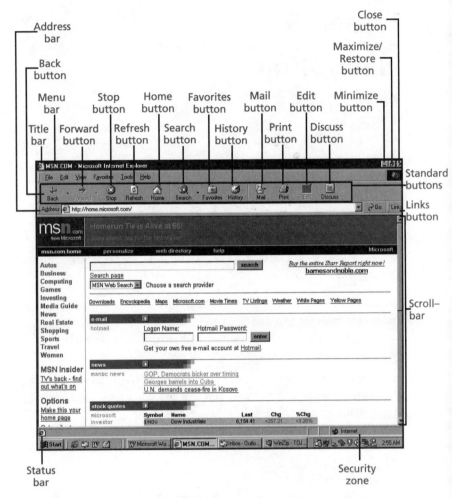

FIGURE 3.1   Anatomy of the Internet Explorer 5 screen.

This appears in the page's title bar.

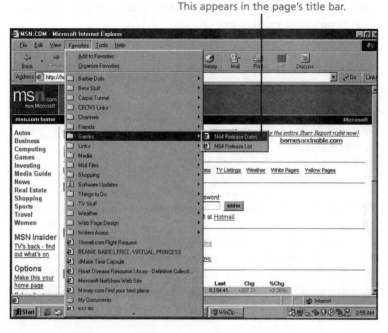

FIGURE 3.2   The information you see here is pulled from the page's title.

It's the Size That Counts

You'll see three buttons at the far right of the title bar: Minimize, Maximize/Restore, and Close.

The Minimize button allows you to "hide" the Internet Explorer window, giving you a clear view of your Windows desktop. To bring the Internet Explorer window back up, simply click its button on the Windows taskbar at the bottom of the screen.

The Maximize/Restore button works like this: When a program opens, it usually has a default screen size. With one click of the Maximize/Restore button, the window will grow to full screen. Click it again, and the window returns to its original size.

Internet Explorer 5 includes the Close button, which is the quickest way to shut down most any Windows program.

What's on the Menu (Bar)?

If you've worked with Windows applications for any amount of time, you'll surely recognize many of the items on Internet Explorer's menu bar. Items such as File, Edit, View, and Help are standards among Windows programs.

The File Menu

The File menu traditionally enables you to open and shut files that are readable in the current application; print the current page or document; or send the page to a specified recipient. This is very much true with Internet Explorer, with the possible exception of opening and closing a document. There are several less cumbersome ways to open and close something in Internet Explorer. That is explained in the "There's More Than One Way to Reach a Web Site" section found later in this lesson.

The Edit Menu

The Edit menu is used to insert and delete text and images on a page as well as cut, copy, and paste various items. Because Internet Explorer is primarily a browsing tool rather than a text editor, Edit menu items are usually limited to copying and pasting bits of text from a Web page to a word processor or Web page authoring tool for future use.

The View Menu

The View menu typically houses commands designed to alter the appearance of the Web page or document you are viewing. You can also toggle toolbars on and off. There are a few additional options in Internet Explorer, however. You can use this menu to refresh a Web page or stop it from loading.

The Help Menu

The Help menu, of course, leads you to a variety of resources, including online documentation and application-specific Web sites maintained by Microsoft. No big surprise here!

The Go and Favorites Menu Items

The two menu items that are unique to Internet Explorer, however, are known as Go and Favorites. The Go menu is a navigational aid that helps you move from one application in the Internet Explorer 5 suite to another. For instance, you can jump to your Outlook Express mail from within Internet Explorer. It also holds the corresponding menu commands for the Back and Forward buttons as well as Search and Home.

We will cover the Favorites menu in excruciating detail in Lesson 5. The favorites menu is where you'll go to access selected Web sites, organize those Web sites, and get them configured for browsing offline.

Back!

The Back button is the first of Internet Explorer's buttons. It's not very complex at all. The Back button will become active once you've browsed more than one Web page, enabling you to go back where you came from one Web page at a time.

If you're really observant, you may have noticed the drop-down arrow immediately to the right of the Back button. This button lets you hop back to any of the last nine Web pages visited in the current session.

About Face! (or Forward)

Take everything you read about the Back button and reverse it—you'll have a description of the Forward button. Though not quite as useful as its counterpart, the Forward button drop-down arrow gives you the same opportunity to leap through cyberspace. Of course, you must have visited several Web sites and moved backward before this button becomes active.

Stop the World (Wide Web), I Wanna Get Off!

There are times when you'll swear a Web page is taking forever to download. I readily admit patience is not my forté, but download lengths get ridiculous at times. That's where the Stop button comes in handy. One press of the button, and Internet Explorer gives up and readies itself for your next assignment.

The Stop button is also a lifesaver when browsing graphic-intensive sites. Since the graphics are often the last things to load on a page, you can stop the page from loading when all of the text appears. That way you can go about your business without coming to a screeching halt.

Freshening Up Your Data

Nothing's worse than old news—especially on the Web, where breaking news is available to all, thanks to a number of news wires.

Why is freshness so critical? Consider these situations: As I write this, it's a stormy summer in the Washington, D.C./Baltimore area. On sweltering afternoons, I like to keep one eye on the local Doppler weather radar in case a nasty thunderstorm is on its way. That way I can save my work and shut down my system before it falls victim to Mother Nature. One quick click of the Refresh button and I'm staring at the freshest data available.

The Refresh button also comes in handy when browsing sports scores, stock information, and online auction sites where data is changed frequently.

 If in doubt, click Refresh! Sometimes Internet Explorer will try to be smart and cache a Web site so it's more readily retrieved. While this optimizes the application's performance, it does so at the expense of occasionally delivering old data. If something doesn't look quite right, click Refresh just to be sure.

Cache   Pronounced *cash*, this term refers to the place in a PC where data is stored so the computer won't have to go out and ask a remote server for it again. While it can be a great performance optimizer, it does have some drawbacks (as described earlier in this chapter).

There's No Place Like Home

It's easy to get lost out there in cyberspace. That's why the Home button is so useful. No matter where you are, you can always click this little button and return to your default home page.

Search Me!

With millions of Web sites out there, finding what you're looking for can be a major challenge. Luckily, there are dozens of powerful search engines ready to come to your rescue. (We'll explore them in detail in Lesson 9, "Finding Sites Online.") Internet Explorer has gone a step further and brought the search engine to you.

Remember when you customized the Internet Start page in the preceding chapter? You were asked to select a primary search provider, among other things. Now you get to see that decision pay off. When you press the Search button, a frame presenting the new Microsoft Search Assistant and your chosen search provider appears on the left side of the screen (see Figure 3.3).

The Search Assistant lets you focus on a specific type of resource such as a map or an encyclopedia. To perform a search within the chosen category, just click inside the text box to set the insertion point, type in your chosen word or phrase, and then click the Search button located in the Search Assistant pane. (Click the button on the toolbar and the search window will vanish faster than you can say, "Hey, who stole my search engine?") A list of sites matching your criteria will be displayed. Just click a site's entry to visit it. To end the search and close the search frame, simply click the Search button on the Internet Explorer 5 toolbar a second time, or click the x in the upper-right corner of the Search Assistant pane.

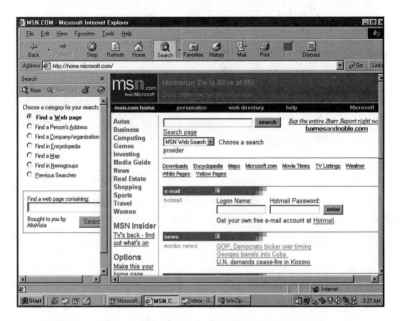

FIGURE 3.3   The new Microsoft Search Assistant helps you home in on what you're looking for.

Playing Favorites Another Way

Internet Explorer 5's Favorites button gives you instant access to the sites you love most. Figure 3.4 shows you what you will see if you click the Favorites button.

A frame, much like the one described in the "Search Me!" section, appears on the left side of the screen. With it you can easily keep browsing the Web while choosing which favorite to visit next. Also notice the Add and Organize buttons at the top of the frame. Now you can easily add new sites to your list—pressing the Add button while a site appears in the main IE viewing area—or organize the ones already residing on your list by clicking the Organize button. (More on dealing with favorites in Lesson 5.)

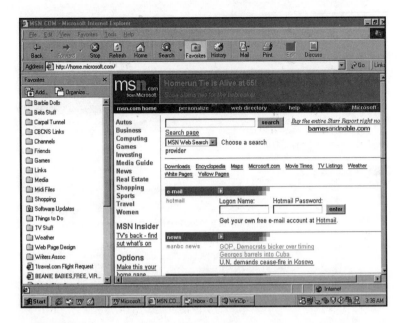

FIGURE 3.4 You can browse your favorites without obstructing the view of the current Web page.

To close the Favorites frame, either click the x at the top-right corner of the Favorites frame or click the **Favorites** button a second time.

Revisiting the Historic Past

Have you ever read something that you wanted to go back and find at a later date only to discover you can't remember where you read it? So maybe the question is a little confusing (or at least its wording is); you'll soon see the merit of this cool History feature.

If you can remember the approximate date you visited the site, you stand a fair shot of finding it again. Just click the History button, press the button that best corresponds to the suspected date (see Figure 3.5), and then glance through the list of sites until you locate an URL that looks familiar. It may take a couple of tries, but you'll find it eventually.

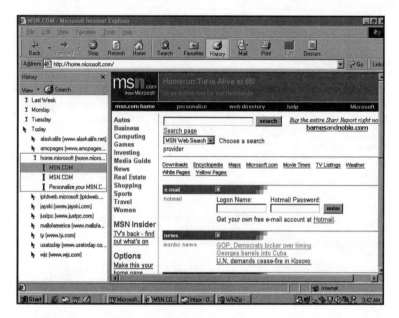

FIGURE 3.5 By default, you can isolate any day over the past week or either of the past two weeks.

If you haven't the time for a leisurely stroll down memory lane, you'll love that View drop-down arrow in the upper-left corner of the History pane. Just click it and point to any of the following special views:

- By Date
- By Site
- By Most Visited
- By Order Visited Today

You can also search the History links by clicking the History pane's **Search** button, or by selecting **Search** from the bottom of the View drop-down menu. Type in a word or words, and Internet Explorer 5 will go back in time and attempt to retrieve what you're looking for.

Getting out of History mode is a snap—just click the **History** button a second time, or click the **x** in the upper-right corner of the History frame.

One-Stop Communications Shop

The Mail button is literally your one-stop communication shop. Mirroring the function of the File menu's Send command, you can check your email, send a buddy a link to a cool page (or send him the whole page if his mail program understands HTML), or scan the newsgroups.

The feature works best with Outlook Express, but other mail programs can be defined. To do this, click **Tools, Internet Options**, and access the **Programs** tab of the Options dialog box. Use the email drop-down box to select from the list of supported email clients. Without Outlook Express, you may not have the ability to send a Web page or browse the news.

I'll go into much greater detail about using the Mail button and its corresponding arrow button in Lesson 6, "Sharing Your Favorite Web Sites."

A Copy for Your Records?

If you've used Microsoft Word or Excel, you'll find it comforting (at least from a familiarity standpoint) to know that the Internet Explorer Print button functions the exact same way as the Print buttons found in those programs. Clicking it gives you one copy of the current page based on all the Print function default settings—nothing fancy. Internet Explorer also has some advanced print settings, which I discuss in great detail in the larger version of this book: *Sams Teach Yourself Microsoft Internet Explorer 5 in 24 Hours*, available at fine book stores everywhere.

Addressing Your Web Browser

Using the Internet Explorer 5 Address bar, you can simply type in the URL you got from a friend, heard on TV or the radio, or read in a newspaper or magazine. While Web addresses need the http:// prefix, Internet Explorer is kind enough to supply it for you. In fact, it even supplies the www and the .com if you simply type a word into the Address bar. Use this technique with caution, though—some Web addresses don't have a www or a .com.

See the Whole Picture

For Web pages that overflow a screen's normal boundaries, Internet Explorer will display both vertical and horizontal scrollbars. Either click the arrows to move in the direction of the arrow or click the scroll box and drag it until the desired elements appear onscreen. If you press the F11 key, you'll enter full screen mode, which gives you additional real estate by removing the toolbars.

Give Me Your Status

Nothing's more frustrating than staring at a motionless computer program and wondering whether it's doing anything. With Internet Explorer, you have multiple ways to determine whether the program is working—or is frozen in its tracks.

The Internet Explorer icon at the top-right corner of the screen moves to show you Internet Explorer is attempting to do something. If that isn't enough reassurance, look down to the status bar at the bottom of the screen. In the left pane of the status bar, you'll find messages such as "Looking up site," "Opening page," and "Connecting to page." Once the page has been reached, a blue status bar appears in the center pane, showing you just how much of the page has been downloaded.

 Where am I going? When you run your mouse pointer over a link (see the following section), the URL will appear in the status bar's left pane. This enables you to see where you're going before you even click a button.

The Security Zone status, which you examine in greater detail in Lesson 8, "Safe, Secure Surfing," is on the far right end of the status bar.

There's More Than One Way to Reach a Web Site

Now that you know where everything is in Internet Explorer 5, it's time to look at how to make your way from page to page. There are oodles of ways to access a Web page or site within Internet Explorer 5. The most fundamental way to reach a site is to follow something called a link.

Link to everything   Think back to your Internet Start page. Each line of text that enables you to jump to another page is underlined and displayed in blue, while standard text appears in black. This blue under-lined text is known as a *link*. Your mouse pointer will also change its appearance when you run it over a link. It will change from the usual arrow to a pointing finger, signaling that you'll be transferred to a new location if you click where the mouse is located.

Picture this   Do you know that images can also con-tain links to new pages? Some pictures, called *imagemaps*, contain multiple links. Run the cursor over different parts of the images to see where the links will take you on the left side of the status bar. In fact, the entire URL will appear on the status bar at the bottom of the screen.

Another way to access a Web page was touched upon during our discussion about the Address bar. It's simply to enter the Web site's address (or URL) in the Address box.

Some additional ways to move from page to page include (but are not limited to) the following:

- Use the Back and Forward buttons. This option works only after you've surfed through a few pages.

- Click a Web site's icon on the Windows desktop. To do this, you first need to create a shortcut to the Web page on your desktop. You can do this one of two ways. If Internet Explorer is in full screen mode, right-click the Web page's display and select the **Create Shortcut** option from the pop-up menu (see Figure 3.6). If you can see part of your Windows desktop, click the page's icon in the Address bar and then drag it to the desktop.

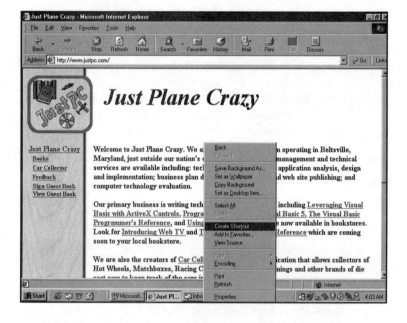

FIGURE 3.6   Choose Create Shortcut from the pop-up menu to access a Web page from your Windows desktop.

- Choose a site from your **Favorites** list, which we'll cover in great detail in Lesson 5.

- If you've visited a Web site previously and begin typing its address into the Address box, Internet Explorer's AutoComplete feature will attempt to guess what you're looking for by displaying a drop-down menu of matching URLs (see Figure 3.7). To accept an AutoComplete selection, simply click it; it will appear onscreen.

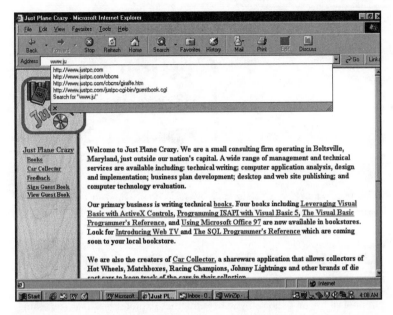

FIGURE 3.7 Internet Explorer 5's AutoComplete feature tries to find what you're looking for.

- Use the History button to relocate recently visited sites, as described earlier in the lesson.

LESSON 4

Getting Help in Internet Explorer 5

This lesson introduces you to many ways Internet Explorer can assist you while you're working with the browser.

Introducing AutoComplete for Forms

In the last lesson I showed you how Internet Explorer taps into something called AutoComplete to help fill in the URL of previously visited Web sites in the Address bar.

You'll routinely come across forms such as the Address bar on Web pages you visit, whether it's a search form at your favorite online bookseller or a basic search engine form. The first time you enter text into a form, Internet Explorer 5 will ask you if you want the Web browser to "remember" your entry. Known as AutoComplete for Forms, this feature, when enabled, will recall entries typed into a given form by displaying a drop-down box of selections much like you see with AutoComplete. To accept a suggestion on a future visit to the same form, double-click it and then click the necessary button to set off the search.

While the feature is tremendously helpful for repeat searches at the same location on the same topic, it can also be an invasion of privacy. Say you're trying to research a personal medical condition or track down an elusive Beanie Baby for your daughter's birthday. Someone who uses the computer after you could see what you've been searching for. That person would have to visit the exact same sites you did, but that's a distinct possibility if you use common search engines.

In response to this potential concern, Microsoft gives you the opportunity
to enable, disable, and clear the AutoComplete feature.

Modifying AutoComplete Forms Settings

To change the way AutoComplete works on your computer, follow these
steps:

1. On the Internet Explorer Tools menu, choose **Internet Options**.

2. Click the **Content** tab to open it.

3. In the Personal Information section of the screen, you'll need to
   click the **AutoComplete** button. The AutoComplete Settings dialog box appears (see Figure 4.1).

FIGURE 4.1   You'll notice that the option to have Internet Explorer
"remember" user IDs and passwords is set on this screen as well.

4. Check or uncheck the **Forms** item as desired (to turn the
   AutoComplete Forms feature on or off).

5. If you want to leave AutoComplete for Forms enabled but want
   to clear your entries, click **Clear Forms**.

6. When you've finished adjusting the settings, click **OK**.

7. Click **Apply** and then **OK** to close the Options dialog box and
   continue working in Internet Explorer.

Hold it right there! Clicking **Clear Forms** will delete everyone's AutoComplete for Forms entries. A better strategy for protecting your privacy might be to turn the feature off when you begin using Internet Explorer and then turn it back on before leaving the application.

 Just when you thought it was safe... Clearing forms or disabling AutoComplete while you're surfing offers you some protection, but it's not foolproof. If you really want to cover your tracks with regard to what sites you have visited, you need to click the **Clear History** button on the General tab of the Internet Options dialog box as well. That keeps the site names and addresses from being traced (or inadvertently stumbled into) via the History list. Exercising the Clear History option may cause problems for others who need to track the sites they have visited, so click it with caution.

Remember Me, IE

As you saw earlier, the AutoComplete dialog box also lets you request that Internet Explorer save user IDs and passwords so that you don't have to remember them each time you revisit a site.

Saving user IDs is especially useful now that the Internet has become so crowded. Why? Because a user ID you choose may already be taken, so you might find yourself increasingly using names and passwords you might not choose if you had your druthers. In addition, user IDs and passwords are becoming the norm rather than the exception because more and more sites are customizing their content.

Is the glass half empty or half full?   While not having to remember every user ID and password you acquire is a definite plus, there's a downside to this convenience—the same potential security issues you encounter with the AutoComplete options. With a saved password, anyone who has access to your computer could make unauthorized purchases using your various e-commerce accounts or, worse yet, snoop into your private business. The Clear Passwords button on the AutoComplete dialog box fixes the immediate risk, but ultimately defeats the purpose of not having to remember and re-key all that information. Only you can decide how valid the risks are, given your particular situation.

So how does IE remember all that stuff?   If you've surfed the Internet before, you may have heard talk of things called *cookies*. While they're not the yummy, edible peanut butter variety, they do appease your appetite for personalized information on demand. Essentially, cookies are tiny files that reside on your computer. When you visit a Web site that makes use of cookie technology, you are asked to supply a number of preferences that are then stored on your machine for retrieval by the site on your next visit. This keeps you from having to answer the same set of questions each time you visit a site. It's sort of like the Internet Start page you personalized—it's just there when you need it. You needn't worry about unauthorized information being transferred from your machine to the Web site; it can only retrieve the information you provided it at the very beginning.

The Help Files

Now that you know how to get Internet Explorer to remember vital information, you'll want to learn how to get help with other things as well.

 Here, there, everywhere!   While the AutoComplete features described here are unique to the Internet Explorer Web browser itself, you'll have access to the same types of help files whether you're working in Internet Explorer, NetMeeting, or even FrontPage Express.

From the Internet Explorer Help menu, select **Contents** and **Index**. This takes you to the screen shown in Figure 4.2.

FIGURE 4.2   There are three distinct ways you can extract help from Internet Explorer's help files.

This is probably the first place you should turn if this book doesn't answer your question. You have three tabs to choose from, each offering a slightly different kind of help. The one you choose depends on your personal needs and preferences for learning. Here are some things that may help you decide which type of help is best for you:

- **Contents**   The Contents tab is somewhat like a book; you click a broad topic as opposed to a specific term. It's a great way to get acquainted with the material when you don't have a specific task or term in mind. (Glance at Figure 4.2 for an idea of what I mean.)

- **Index**   The Index tab (shown in Figure 4.3) is just like going to the back of a book to locate a term. The bad news is you have to know what you're looking for. Microsoft does its best to help you, however. Many terms are cross-referenced, and as you type in each letter, the AutoComplete feature quickly takes you to the part of the index you want.

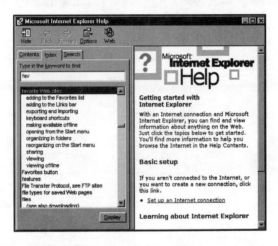

FIGURE 4.3   AutoComplete shoots you directly to the part of the index you're looking for, beginning with the first letter you type.

- **Search**   The Search tab returns a list of topics related to the term you type in (see Figure 4.4). Because it also fetches topics without the term in its title (it does a full-text search), you'll find some extremely useful information with this method.

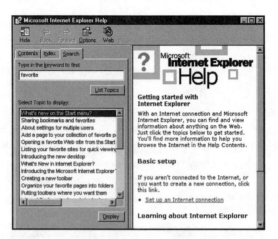

FIGURE 4.4   Learn everything you want about a topic by doing a full-text search of the Help files.

All Kinds of Helpful Goodies

You can access a ton of goodies from the Internet Explorer Help file. You can hop on to Microsoft's Online Support for supplemental help information or view the latest product updates. You can also check out the Microsoft on the Web section to browse the Frequently Asked Questions about Internet Explorer 5 or download some free stuff (such as additional Outlook Express stationery or browser power tools as they become available).

This lesson gave you an overview of the many ways Internet Explorer can help you go about your business on the Web with minimal hassle. Given all that convenience, you're bound to come across some sites you'll want to be able to access more quickly. In Internet Explorer, these sites are aptly called *favorites*. Working with those favorite Web sites is the focus of your next lesson.

LESSON 5
Working with Your Favorite Web Sites

This lesson brings you up to speed on saving, organizing, and visiting your favorite sites on the Web.

What Is a Favorite?

After you've been around the Internet for awhile, you'll start to see that there are three kinds of Web sites:

- Those that are of no interest to you (or are so useless that they're not worth revisiting).

- Those that contain interesting content that doesn't get updated very often (or sites you use occasionally to search for specific information).

- Those you visit weekly (if not daily) for the most current information.

Of these, the last group makes up an elite list of what typically is referred to as Favorites (or Bookmarks, if you're a Netscape user).

Should I Really Save It as a Favorite?

When you start surfing for the first time, the natural instinct is to save just about every interesting site you come across as a Favorite. While it may seem like a good idea at the time, doing so could have serious consequences. Granted your system won't roll over and gasp for its last breath, but *you* may, as you try to weed through dozens of Web sites that have evolved into one horrendous mess of a Favorites list.

So which Web sites should you save as Favorites? Keep in mind that you can effortlessly organize the sites into folders for easy access. Beyond that, here are some things that may help you make a decision:

- Does the Web site have an easy–to–remember address? Web sites like www.cbs.com are a breeze to remember, so you may find re-keying them a whole lot easier (and faster) than sifting through scads of Favorites links. Sites best suited for the Favorites list are those that go something like www.wam.umd.edu/~wfreeze. They tend to be the hardest to remember.

- Do you access the site regularly? If you access it less than once a month, it may not be worth cluttering up your Favorites list. If, on the other hand, you visit a site once a week or even daily, it may very well be a good candidate for your Favorites list.

- Remember AutoComplete—Internet Explorer's ability to "guess" what you want to type based on the first few letters you type. This can be an extremely viable alternative to the Favorites list when the number of sites on the list starts to get out of control.

Now that you've got some criteria to help you determine whether or not you want to enter a certain site into that coveted list, let's learn how to save a site as a Favorite.

Saving a Web Site as a Favorite

To begin creating your list of favorite Web sites, follow these simple steps:

1. When you come upon a site you want to save to your Favorites list, right-click anywhere on the page. A pop-up menu (also called a shortcut menu) like the one in Figure 5.1 will open.

FIGURE 5.1 The shortcut menu is the quickest way to begin saving a page as a Favorite.

2. Select **Add to Favorites** from the list. A dialog box like the one shown in Figure 5.2 will appear.

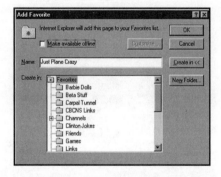

FIGURE 5.2 Soon your Favorites dialog box will have as many folders as this one!

3. If the Web page has a defined title, it will appear in the Name box. If it doesn't (or if you'd rather call it something else), simply click inside the **Name** box and type in the new name.

4. Once the page's name meets with your approval, click **OK**. The page will be saved to your default Favorites folder until you define new folders and move it elsewhere.

Your folders look better than mine!   Internet Explorer 5 comes with four riveting Favorites folders predefined: Channels, Links, Media, and Software Updates. While your set of folders in the Create In box may look boring now, just wait. In a few minutes, I'll have you creating new Favorites folders of your own!

Viewing a Favorite

You can view a favorite Web site one of two ways. Click the **Favorites** button on the menu bar and then select the desired site; or click the **Favorites** button and click the desired link in the frame on the left side of the screen.

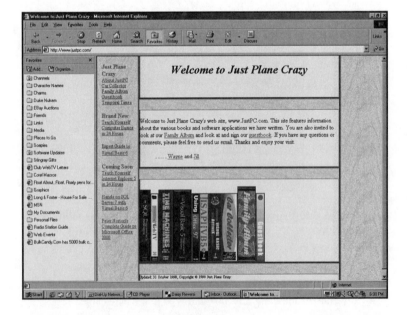

FIGURE 5.3   Skim through your Favorites and surf at the same time!

Please note that when your Favorites list is organized into folders, you may first have to click a folder to open it, and then click the site itself.

Creating a Shortcut to a Web Site on Your Windows Desktop

Internet Explorer 5 gives you the opportunity to make your favorite Web sites even more easily accessible by creating shortcut icons for the pages on your Windows desktop. The way you do it depends on whether or not you can see the Windows desktop with Internet Explorer running.

If you can see a portion of the desktop, you can create a shortcut icon to the page on your desktop by following these steps:

1. Load the desired Web page so it's active in Internet Explorer.

2. Click the Web page's icon located on the Address bar next to its URL.

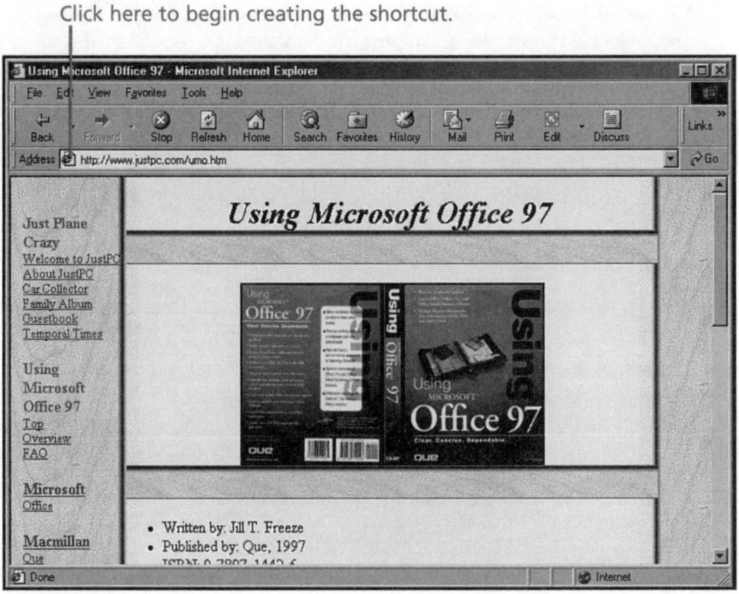

Click here to begin creating the shortcut.

FIGURE 5.4   Creating a shortcut to your Favorites is a simple click and drag process.

3. Holding the left mouse button down, drag the icon to an open space on your desktop.

4. When the icon is where you want it, release the mouse button. You're done!

5. To view this page, all you'll have to do is double-click its icon on your desktop. It's as simple as that.

If none of the desktop is visible, you can follow these steps to create a shortcut:

1. With the desired Web page open, right-click the page (you don't need to choose the page's icon here; the viewing area is fine). The shortcut menu shown in Figure 5.1 appears.

2. Select **Create Shortcut** from the menu.

 My web page doesn't have that on the menu! Don't panic. If the mouse pointer was over an image, you may get the shortcut menu enabling you to cut and copy the element or whatever. If this happens, try clicking elsewhere on the page, preferably in a location without graphics. That should rectify the problem. This may not happen to you all the time. It just seems that, for whatever reason, some Web pages are more finicky than others.

3. Internet Explorer will ask you to verify that you want to create the shortcut to this Web page on your Windows desktop (see Figure 5.5). Click **OK** or **Cancel** as appropriate.

FIGURE 5.5 Click OK if you want the shortcut icon to appear on your Windows desktop.

Organizing Your Favorite Web Sites

As you venture around the information superhighway, your list of
Favorites may grow at a surprising rate. As a result, you'll need to do
some virtual spring cleaning. There are multiple steps involved in organizing your Favorites, as you'll see next.

1. With Internet Explorer up and running, choose **Organize
    Favorites** from the Favorites menu. The Organize Favorites dia-
    log box pictured in Figure 5.6 will open.

FIGURE 5.6   Welcome to Favorites headquarters! Soon you'll have
as many defined folders as you see here.

2. The first thing you'll need to do is create some folders. Try to
    lump your Favorites into specific categories like Cats, Work
    Stuff, Job Hunting, or whatever. When you have some good
    folder names in mind, click the **Create Folder** button.

3. A new folder appears at the bottom of the screen. Its blue high-
    light prompts you to enter a name for it. Type in the chosen
    name, and then click **Return**. The folder has been created.

4. Repeat the process until all your favorite Web pages have a logi-
    cal home.

5. Now comes the fun part—moving the pages to their new homes.
    Click the first link in your list of Favorites.

6. Click the Move to Folder button to bring up the Browse for Folder dialog box shown in Figure 5.7.

FIGURE 5.7   This box displays each of the new folders you created.

7. Click the folder to which you wish to move the selected page, and then click OK.

8. The selected item will now appear in its new folder. Repeat the process of selecting a link and moving it until all of the links have a home.

9. To see which pages are located within a folder, click the folder once. The page titles will appear underneath their new home. Click the folder again to "hide" the pages.

10. If you want the folders to appear in an order other then alphabetical, you'll have to move them by clicking a folder and then repeatedly clicking Move Up or Move Down until the folder is in the desired location.

11. When everything's in order, click the Close button to close the dialog box.

Now you have a neat and tidy list of Favorites that's easy to ..avigate.

Deleting a Favorites Page

To delete a Favorites page from your list permanently, do the following:

1. With Internet Explorer up and running, choose **Organize Favorites** from the Favorites menu. The familiar Organize Favorites dialog box appears.

2. Click the link you wish to delete, and then click the **Delete** button.

3. Internet Explorer will ask you to confirm the request to delete the item, as shown in Figure 5.8. Click **Yes** if you wish to remove it or **No** if you discovered you made an error.

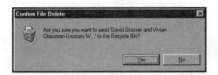

FIGURE 5.8   Click **Yes** if you wish to make the deletion official.

The page is now out of your sight for good, making room for new Favorites on your list.

In this lesson, you learned all the basics entailed in saving, organizing, and accessing your favorite Web sites. Next up is how to share those favorites.

LESSON 6

Sharing Your Favorite Web Sites

Whether you want to send your list of favorite stingray sites to your brother in Massachusetts or you need to take work-related links into your Netscape machine at work, this lesson will prepare you for the task.

Sharing Your Favorite Web Sites

With Internet Explorer, there are several ways to share your favorite Web sites with family, friends, and associates. They include

- Emailing the link to the Web page

- Sending the entire Web page

- Exporting your entire Favorites list

- Exporting a single folder full of goodies

- Sending the page as an HTML file attachment

- Importing Favorites sent to you by others (or transferring your Favorites from work to your home machine)

We will cover each of these operations in detail in the sections that follow.

Emailing a Link to a Web Page

Follow these steps to send someone a link to one of your favorite sites:

1. While you're browsing the page you want to share, go to the **File** menu, select **Send**, and then **Link by E-mail**. Internet Explorer will launch Outlook Express (or whatever default email

client you've defined) to assist with the task. The subject line will be filled in, and the link will already be printed as an attachment to the message.

2. Type in the desired email address (or use the Outlook Express Address Book as described in Lesson 11, "Sending Email with Outlook Express"), and then click **Send**. The lucky recipient will receive a message similar to the one shown in Figure 6.1 (assuming he or she is using Outlook Express).

FIGURE 6.1 Here is what the outgoing link message will look like.

Emailing the Entire Web Page

Use these steps to send the whole Web page to a recipient:

1. Browse to the Web page you wish to send.

2. Click the **File** menu and select **Send, Page by E-Mail**.

3. Internet Explorer will launch Outlook Express (or your alternate default email client) and give you an opportunity to fill in the recipient's email address.

Hey, whatya mean I can't send that? Just because books, artwork, music, and so on are available free online doesn't mean they are copyright free—free for the taking. It's possible that if you try to send a page of material that's password protected or protected by some other measure, you may see a message that says you are unable to send the material. There is no workaround here; the prospective recipient will either have to access the site himself and register for a password or settle for a summary of the information from you.

4. When everything's ready to go, click **Send**. Output similar to Figure 6.2 will be sent to the recipient's email account. Note that the recipient may need to maximize his or her email screen to see the page in its full glory.

FIGURE 6.2 Sending the entire Web page is one way to be sure your recipient checks out the page.

Exporting Your Favorites List

Say you're getting a new computer and are handing your old one down to the kids. Wouldn't it be great if you could take your Favorites list with you? Follow these quick steps to get the job done:

1. From within Internet Explorer 5, click File, Import and Export. The Import/Export Wizard appears (see Figure 6.3). Click Next to begin.

FIGURE 6.3   The Import/Export Wizard is your starting point for exchanging Favorites.

    Take it easy   Maybe you don't want to share your entire Favorites list, but just a special folder or subfolder of interest to the recipient. You can do that by clicking the Choose Folder button seen back in Figure 6.2, and then double-clicking the name of the folder you wish to export or share. Only that folder will be passed along.

2. Choose Export Favorites from the list of possible actions, and then click Next.

3. Next, you will need to choose the folder you'd like to export. Just click it, and then click Next. Please note that you can only export one folder at a time.

4. The Export Favorites Destination screen gives you two options: 1) to export your Internet Explorer 5 Favorites to another Web browser on your system (like Netscape), or 2) to save it to a file location by clicking the Browse button. When you've located the spot, give the file a descriptive, easy-to-remember name such as Shopping or Cat Favs. Internet Explorer will automatically save it as an HTML file with an .htm file extension. When you've made your selection, click Next.

 Where should I put it? If you plan to take the file to work, you may want to cut a disk containing the file, which will mean using the A: drive. If you're connected to a LAN or similar network, consider saving the file to one of the shared directories for easy retrieval. If you plan to email the file to yourself or somebody else, just tuck it away in an easy-to-remember spot on your C: drive.

5. The wizard will display a message saying that you've successfully completed the Import/Export Wizard. All you need to do is click Finish to complete the process. A small dialog box appears saying that the export was successful. Click OK to close the wizard.

Importing Those Favorite Links

Now it's time to get those imported Favorites where they belong—back on a computer. Follow these steps to import Favorites into another copy of Internet Explorer:

1. On Internet Explorer's File menu, select Import and Export. The Import/Export Wizard launches. Click Next to begin the process.

2. Next, you will need to select **Import Favorites** from the list of actions provided, and then click **Next**.

3. Browse to the location in which the Favorites list was saved. It may be your A: drive if you transported the list via disk, or a location you specified when you retrieved the list from your mail server.

4. When you find the file, double-click it, and then click the **Next** button.

5. At this point, you may specify a folder under which to nest the imported favorites by clicking it; otherwise, its own folder will be created. Click **Next** to proceed.

6. A message displays, saying you're about to complete the wizard. Click **Finish** to make it official. A small dialog box appears saying the import was executed. Click **OK** to acknowledge the dialog and dismiss the wizard.

But what about Netscape?   As mentioned, these HTML files can be imported into Netscape as well, but you'll need to consult the procedures in the help files of the target version of Netscape for the most up-to-date, step-by-step directions.

Dealing with Email Sharing

To perform the export/import via email, there are some things you'll need to know. First, the export is performed exactly as described previously in this lesson. To send it via email, you'll need to launch Outlook Express (or your email client of choice), begin composing a new message, click the **Paperclip** icon, and browse to the desired HTML file to attach it to the message. If you don't use Outlook Express for email, the procedure for attaching the file will differ.

If you're on the receiving end of a Favorites list passed on by email, you'll have to save the file attachment somewhere on your computer before you can perform the import as described earlier.

In this lesson, you learned everything you need to know to share your favorite Web sites with others, even if it's just with yourself on another machine. In the next lesson, we'll turn our attention to another neat feature—offline browsing.

LESSON 7
Browsing Web Sites Offline

If you've ever wished you could browse your favorite Web sites without being tied down to a phone line, you'll be excited by the contents of this lesson.

Why Browse Web Sites Offline?

Are you tired of battling over time online? Are your friends and family tired of getting busy signals every time they try to call you? Do you wish you could get caught up with all the news on the Internet during your long train ride to work? If any of these situations describe you, you'll be thrilled to learn more about how you can enjoy your favorite Web site without being linked to the Internet.

With Internet Explorer 5, it's easy to make a Web page available offline. The exact method you use will vary slightly, depending on whether or not the site has been previously saved as a Favorite.

Saving a Web Page as a Favorite and Making It Available Offline

For Web pages not currently saved as Favorites on your system, follow these steps to make them available offline:

1. With the desired Web page onscreen, right-click inside the page's viewing area to open the shortcut menu. Select **Add to Favorites** to open the Add Favorites dialog box.

2. Place a check mark in the Make Available Offline box as shown in Figure 7.1.

Click here to make the page available offline.

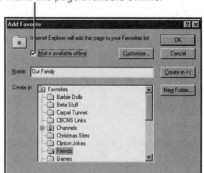

FIGURE 7.1   One click is all it takes to make a page available offline.

3. If you want the page to have scheduled automatic updates, click the **Customize** button. This will launch the Offline Favorite Wizard, shown in Figure 7.2. This is the easiest way to schedule an automatic synchronization, so it's worth considering.

 Automatic Synchronization   When a Web page is automatically synchronized, it means that Internet Explorer will download an updated copy of the page at the time you specify.

4. On the Welcome screen, you can place a check mark in the check box to keep the wizard from displaying its introduction screen each time you use it. Click **Next** to continue.

5. The next screen reiterates the page you've selected to make available offline and asks if you want to save any of the pages that may be linked to the selected page. Unless you have disk space to burn, you may want to say **No**. Click **Next** to move to the next step.

FIGURE 7.2   Presenting the Offline Favorite Wizard, the easiest way to define synchronization options.

6. You must now decide how and when you want the page synchronized (see Figure 7.3). Choose the first option when you want to synchronize on demand only (manual synchronization). The second option lets you totally control the times of your automatic synchronization. Click Next to proceed.

Your options increase   If you've used this procedure to make a schedule before, you'll see three options instead of two in the dialog box shown in Figure 7.3. That's because Internet Explorer 5 lets you lump the current site's schedule in with one defined at an earlier date. That way your computer isn't constantly trying to perform synchronizations at various times.

7. If you opted to create your own schedule, you'll be led through the screen shown in Figure 7.4. Use the drop-down arrows to select the frequency and time for the synchronization, and then type in a name for the schedule before clicking Next.

FIGURE 7.3 Choose the method of synchronization that works best for you.

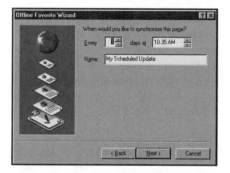

FIGURE 7.4 Define the frequency and time for your schedule, and give it a name.

8. If you've created a schedule, you'll be taken directly to a screen that asks whether or not a username and password are required to retrieve the site (see Figure 7.5). Once you've entered the user ID and password, click **Finish**.

9. Click the folder in which you wish to store the Favorite, and then click **OK** to complete the request. Internet Explorer 5 will perform its first synchronization on the spot so you have a fresh version of the chosen page on your local machine. The Synchronizing dialog box, shown in Figure 7.6, keeps you apprised of the status of the synchronization.

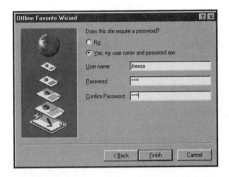

FIGURE 7.5   If a password is required, click Yes, and then enter the necessary information.

FIGURE 7.6   The Synchronizing screen keeps you up–to–date on the status of the download.

You'll learn more about scheduling synchronizations later in the lesson.

Making a Favorite Site Available Offline

For sites already saved to your Favorites list, follow these steps:

1. From Internet Explorer's File menu, select Organize Favorites. The Organize Favorites dialog box appears.

2. Click the title of the Web site you wish to make available offline.

3. Click the Make Available Offline check box as shown in Figure 7.7, and then click Close to complete the transaction.

Why work through the Offline Favorite Wizard if you want to do manual synchronizations? It's true that you can select a page to be manually synchronized by simply checking its Make Available Offline check box. If that page is password protected, the Offline Favorite Wizard can remember the password for you so you don't have to manually enter it after each manual synchronization.

If you work with a lot of secure sites, the wizard will save you time in the long run and will be a lot less distracting, too, because each site won't have to prompt you for a user ID and password. There is a potential security risk here, however. Once that secure page is on your machine, anyone who has access to your machine can browse to it. Only you know how much of a security threat really exists in your particular work environment.

And remember, not all sites that request user ID and password information present a potential security hazard. Some sites request this information to generate customized sites based on preferences you expressed previously. News sites and last-minute travel sites immediately come to mind.

Click here to make the selected Favorite available offline.

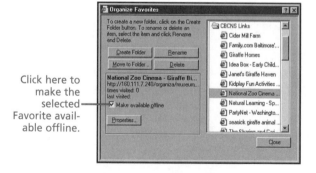

Figure 7.7 One click now makes old Favorites available anytime!

Clicking the OK button in either case will prompt Internet Explorer to synchronize your offline Web sites so you have the most current version available (see Figure 7.8). This initial synchronization takes place to store a copy of the page on your system. Internet Explorer 5 uses this information later to determine whether it needs to download a fresh copy of the page.

FIGURE 7.8   A status bar lets you know how much waiting time is left.

Manually Synchronizing Your Offline Favorites

Unless you have a full-time connection to the Internet or are willing to spend lots of time configuring update schedules, you may find that manually synchronizing your chosen Web pages works best for you.

You get out of it what you put into it   I know it's another tired cliché, but it's very applicable in this case. Manually synchronizing your files is fun and useful in some ways, but for the ultimate in offline convenience, you'll want to schedule regular updates to the selected pages. You can learn how to "surf while you sleep" by reading *Sams Teach Yourself Internet Explorer 5 in 24 Hours*.

To get the most up-to-date copies of your selected Favorites, click the Internet Explorer Tools menu item and select Synchronize. A window like the one shown in Figure 7.9 will open, enabling you to place a check mark next to the items you want to have synchronized. Select

Synchronize or Close as desired. Be forewarned, however, that the synchronization process may take a bit longer than you anticipate. The status
bar will keep you apprised of the situation and will alert you to any problems it may encounter.

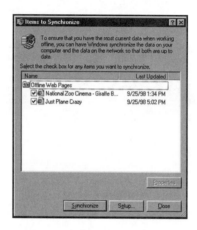

FIGURE 7.9   Check the items you want to synchronize.

Once the job is done, a Synchronization Complete status window will
appear (see Figure 7.10). It tells you whether or not there were any problems with the download. And, if you click the Details button and look in
the Results tab, you'll see which pages were updated with new content.

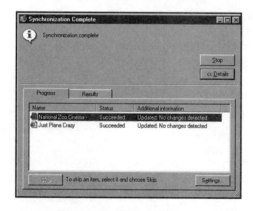

FIGURE 7.10   The Synchronization Complete window delivers the
results of the synchronization.

Viewing Your Favorite Pages Offline

Okay, you know how to mark a page for offline viewing and how to synchronize it. But how in the world do you view it? Just follow these quick steps:

1. Without connecting to the Internet, launch Internet Explorer.

2. The dialog box shown in Figure 7.11 appears, asking whether or not you wish to work offline. Select **Work Offline**. (Of course, this screen will not appear if you connect to the Internet through your office LAN.)

FIGURE **7.11** Press Work Offline to begin your adventure.

3. Next, click the **Favorites** menu item and drag the mouse down until you find the page you want to view. If it is available offline, it will load as usual.

If you inadvertently choose a site that you've not configured to view offline, Internet Explorer will display the dialog box shown in Figure 7.12.

Should you decide that you want to make the content that produced the error available offline as well, establish a connection to the Internet, and then go back online by clicking Internet Explorer's **File** menu item and deselecting **Work Offline**. You'll need to take steps to make it available offline as described earlier.

FIGURE 7.12   Choose **Connect** to have Internet Explorer download the most current content from the site or **Stay Offline** to retry your request.

If you're certain you made the content available offline, link up to the Internet and click **Tools, Synchronize**. If the item in question appears on that list, try accessing it again. If it doesn't appear on the list, redefine its offline availability as described earlier.

There's even more to offline browsing than you've seen here; we've only begun to scratch the surface. But hopefully you can find a way to enhance your productivity and enjoyment by tapping into this exciting new feature. In the next lesson, we'll take a close look at Internet security.

LESSON 8

Safe, Secure Surfing

This lesson introduces you to the topic of Internet security and shows you how to protect children from inappropriate content.

Dispelling the Myths of Online Security

One of the biggest—if not *the* biggest—fears people have about the Internet is their security. Will someone steal their identity? Will their children stumble onto the seamy side of the Internet and view all kinds of inappropriate content? Will a horrible computer virus be unleashed on their system, causing total computer meltdown? Will their credit card information be intercepted by a crook just waiting to go on a mega shopping spree?

The $10,000 question is, "Are you less safe on the Internet than you are in the real world?" If you listen to the news, you're probably already nodding your head yes. If you're not yet convinced that's the case, read on. I think you'll find some compelling reasons to reserve judgment on the big, bad Internet!

Defining Security Zones

For your protection, Internet Explorer divides your Internet world into four security zones. This enables you to specify varying levels of security, depending on the site and how well you feel you can trust it. These zones carry with them levels of security ranging from low to high. What exactly does this mean? Basically, the higher the level of security, the more warnings you get before you can download something potentially harmful to your computer. In fact, the highest level of security essentially prohibits you from accessing anything dangerous. Of course that can dramatically affect your Web surfing fun, but it may be the best way to put your mind at ease if you're particularly fearful about getting on the Internet. On the flip side, overly cautious settings can actually stifle your Internet experience by disabling some of the more technical capabilities like cookies (which help a Web site "remember" your preferences) and ActiveX controls (which can help you interact with a site).

It's not my default!   While it's true these security zones have default security levels, you can always upgrade or downgrade them as you feel necessary. Or if you're really adventurous, you can customize the settings to cover your most feared areas.

The four Internet Explorer security zones carry the following names:

- **Internet Zone**   The default security zone that carries a Medium security level.

- **Local Intranet Zone**   A Medium security zone designated for sites on your company's intranet. This is also the cluster into which the sites listed in your Connections tab for dialup access fall by default.

- **Trusted Sites Zone**   With its Low security setting, this should be reserved for sites you trust entirely.

- **Restricted Sites Zone**   A High security level designation reserved for sites you're not sure you can trust at all.

The know zone   If you're not sure what zone a certain Web site has been assigned, remember that you can look on the right end of the status bar to find the answer any time you want.

Setting the Level of Security

Internet Explorer gives you the flexibility to assign levels of security to the various zones. If you think the settings should be adjusted, simply do the following:

1. With Internet Explorer up and running, click the **Tools** menu item and select **Internet Options**.

2. Choose the **Security** tab to reveal the screen shown in Figure 8.1.

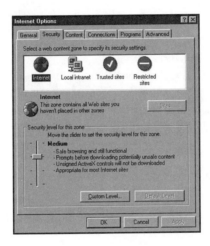

FIGURE 8.1 The Security tab is where you can redefine the levels of security within each zone.

3. Click the name of the security zone you want to edit.

4. Click and drag the slider up or down to reflect the level of security you want to define for the specified site. In case you're not sure what each level means, a full description will appear to the immediate right of the slider.

5. Click **Apply** to save your changes, and then click **OK** to exit the dialog box.

Leave well enough alone   At first glance, Medium security may not seem high enough for the Internet in general. While that may be true in part, bumping the security level up to High may be overkill. Large chunks of the Internet will not be available to you, and your surfing time will constantly be interrupted with various warnings and cautions.

Assigning a Site to a Specific Zone

As you get more and more comfortable with the Internet, you may find you want to change the default zone for a site. For example, with the default Internet Zone setting, you have to go through a series of dialog boxes each time you download a new Internet Explorer component. What a pain! If you make Microsoft a Trusted site, you can download to your heart's content quickly and easily.

Follow these simple steps to change a specific Web site's security zone:

1. From within Internet Explorer's **Tools** menu, select **Internet Options**.

2. Click the **Security** tab to display the dialog box seen back in Figure 8.1.

3. Choose the security zone you want to work with by clicking it.

Why can't I pick the Internet Zone?   Because all sites are placed here by default, you needn't do anything to place a site in this zone.

4. Click the **Sites** button to begin entering the list of sites you want to place in the selected security zone.

5. Type the Web site's URL in the **Add This Web Site to the Zone** box (see Figure 8.2).

6. Unless you're certain that every site on the list operates through a secure server, you'll need to remove the check mark in the **Require Server Verification** box. If you don't, sites on the list not using a secure server will be unavailable.

FIGURE 8.2   Type the desired URL into the **Add This Web Site to the Zone** box.

 How can I tell a site uses a secure server?   Internet Explorer will tell you. Look on the right side of the status bar; if you see a padlock like the one shown in the next figure, you're on a secure server. You may also be able to tell by the presence of a non-http:// prefix in the Address Bar. Secure sites might use shttp:// or https://.

So why should you care if a server is secure? First of all, it protects your credit card number and other personal information from being intercepted over the Internet during e-commerce transactions. A secure server essentially scrambles your information so it can only be interpreted at the receiving end. It does not, however, guarantee that material found there will be suitable for all ages and tastes. You'll need to call on the Content Advisor for that, as you'll see later on in this lesson.

7. Click Add to add the site to your list. Click OK, and the Trusted Sites Zone tab (or whatever zone you're working with) will close.

8. Click OK again to exit the Security tab.

 Zoning out To remove a site from the newly assigned zone, follow steps one through four. Next, click the URL you want to remove, and then click the Remove button. Press OK to complete the request, and then press OK again to close the Security tab.

Protecting Children from Inappropriate Content

While the Internet hosts tons of valuable (and fun) information, some of what you might find may be inappropriate viewing material for young eyes. Let's get real, some of it may even be offensive to many of the adults among us. Luckily there are ways to sift some of it out.

Many Web sites have a defined RSAC (Recreational Software Advisory Council) rating based on the presence (or lack thereof) of language, nudity, sex, and violence. This Internet content rating system is based on more than 20 years of research by Dr. Donald F. Roberts from Stanford University.

Internet Explorer's Content Advisor uses the RSAC ratings information to help you control the content viewed on your computer.

Setting Up the Content Advisor

To get the Content Advisor ready for use, follow these steps:

1. With Internet Explorer up and running, click the Tools menu and select Internet Options.

2. Select the Content tab to reveal the dialog box shown in Figure 8.3.

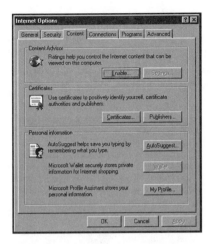

FIGURE 8.3   The Content tab is where you'll begin setting up the Content Advisor.

3. To get started, click the **Enable** button in the Content Advisor section of the tab. You will be taken to the Content Advisor Ratings tab, shown in Figure 8.4.

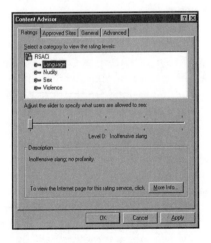

FIGURE 8.4   The Content Advisor Ratings tab is where you'll define how much or how little of each potentially offensive category you will tolerate.

4. Each of the four elements has five levels of adjustability (refer to Table 8.1 to see what each level of each element means). Click the element you wish to adjust, and then move the slider in the desired direction (see Figure 8.5). By default, each element will be disallowed altogether (set to 0).

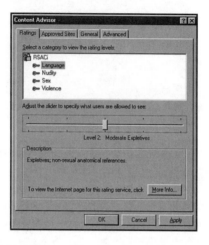

FIGURE 8.5 Click and drag the slider to define your level of tolerance for each element.

 Know what you're ruling out   You should be aware that keeping all settings at the default level may even keep you from seeing such things as news sites or video game sites. Use the child's age and interests as a guide when selecting your settings. Your ten-year-old who loves playing Duke Nukem (a 3D shoot 'em up game) may be kept from visiting sites devoted to the game at Level 1; Level 3 may give him just enough freedom to do so. You're the best judge of what your child can handle and what offends you. At the same time, you need to be aware that ultraconservative settings may make the Internet virtually useless for surfing.

Confused? Don't be! If Table 8.1 still doesn't help you, never fear. As you drag the slider, a brief description of what it filters out appears onscreen.

TABLE 8.1   RSAC Rating Levels Within Each Element

Element	Level 1	Level 2	Level 3	Level 4	Level 5
Language	Inoffensive slang	Mild expletives	Moderate expletives	Obscene gestures	Explicit/ crude language
Nudity	None	Revealing attire	Partial nudity	Frontal nudity	Provocative frontal nudity
Sex	No sexual activity/ romance	Passionate kissing	Clothed sexual touching touching	Non-explicit sexual	Explicit sexual activity
Violence	No violence	Fighting	Killing	Killing with blood and gore	Wanton and gratuitous violence

5. Next, click the Content Advisor's **General** tab. On this tab, pictured in Figure 8.6, you set User Options and can change the supervisor password. By default, users cannot see sites without ratings because this box is not selected. I suggest you leave it this way. Because not all sites are RSAC rated, it'd be easy for children to find inappropriate material. The second option specifies that the supervisor password can be entered on-the-fly to grant access to disallowed content. By default, you are able to do this.

6. Click **Apply**, and then click **OK** when all your settings are complete.

7. Internet Explorer will then ask you to select a password for the Content Advisor. After all, what good is it if anyone can go in and alter the settings? Also, be prepared to type the password twice as a means of verification.

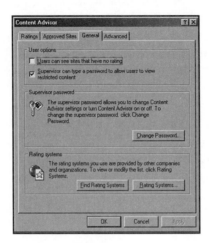

FIGURE 8.6   The General tab is where you'll define some of the higher-level Content Advisor security options.

8. Click **OK** to close the Password dialog box. A message saying the Content Advisor is now enabled will appear.

9. Click **OK** to close the message box.

10. Click **OK** again to close the Internet Options dialog box.

11. Shut down Internet Explorer to clear the cache of previously viewed material, and then launch the application to begin surfing with the Content Advisor in place.

When a user attempts to access a disallowed site, the box in Figure 8.7 appears.

Notice that you have the option to enter the password and click **OK** or click **Cancel** to leave the site.

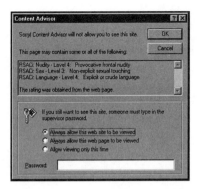

FIGURE 8.7   When you surf to a disallowed site, this box greets you.

Disabling the Content Advisor

Regaining the full run of the Internet without losing your Content Advisor settings is a breeze. Just follow these steps to turn off the Content Advisor:

1. Open Internet Explorer's Tools menu and select Internet Options.

2. Choose the Content tab.

3. To turn off the Content Advisor, click the Disable button in the Content Advisor section of the tab.

4. You'll then need to provide the Content Advisor supervisor password.

5. Click OK to complete the request. Internet Explorer displays the message in Figure 8.8 saying the Content Advisor has been disabled. It also reminds you to turn it back on before letting others use the system.

To enable it again, all you have to do is repeat these steps, clicking the Enable button in step 3.

FIGURE 8.8   This message tells you the Content Advisor has been turned off.

Changing Content Advisor Settings

Any number of circumstances might prompt you to tweak the Content Advisor. Maybe you find that the levels you set for certain elements were too high, thus granting your child access to stronger content than you want. Or maybe your children's ages span from 8 to 18, and you want to regulate each of them differently. Whatever the case, you'll need to follow these steps to make any changes to your Content Advisor settings:

1. Open Internet Explorer's **Tools** menu and select **Internet Options**.

2. Choose the **Content** tab.

3. In the Content Advisor section of the tab, click the **Settings** button.

4. Once again you'll need to provide the Content Advisor supervisor password.

5. Click **OK** to begin making your adjustments.

The options you'll have are identical to the ones described in the "Setting Up the Content Advisor" section earlier in the lesson. Just remember to click **Apply** and **OK** when you're done.

Hopefully you feel a little safer cruising the Internet after this brief lesson. Now let's have some fun and discover how to find what we want on the Information Superhighway.

LESSON 9

Finding Sites Online

This lesson shows you how to find the information you want when you want it online.

How Do I Find the Good Stuff?

With millions of Web pages and well over ten thousand newsgroups out there, it's a wonder anyone finds anything at all! Sure there's something for everyone, but finding that "something" can take a whole lot of time and energy unless you know where—and how—to look.

There are a number of ways you can uncover the good stuff on your travels through the Information Superhighway. Some of the most common include the following:

- **Start here**   From the Microsoft Internet Start page (or whatever page you're currently browsing), click your way through a maze of links that take you to some great hidden information.

- **Follow that sign**   Some of the more frequently visited sites on the Internet sell advertising in the form of colorful, rectangular banner ads. The ads often feature come-on lines to get you to click the rectangle and be transported to the site. Occasionally the click is worth your while, but you never know until you try.

- **A friend of a friend of a friend...**   A buddy of yours may surf to a really cool site and give you its address to check out. This can be one of the best sources of good information. This method can also be extended to include the reference of Web sites in a newsgroup you trust.

- **I saw it on the tube**   With the increasing number of corporations and organizations online, you often see references to Web
page addresses on the television news and commercials, as well
as in a variety of printed media. While that's by no means a tes-
tament to its quality, you can often access a wealth of information about a favorite product this way.

- **The old guessing game**   Say, for instance, you're interested in
buying a new Toyota 4-Runner, but you want to learn more
about its specifications. Rather than query a search engine for
Toyota 4-Runner, you may decide to guess its URL and type
www.toyota.com into Internet Explorer's Address Bar. You'll be
surprised how often the old guessing game actually works.

- **From Web sites you can trust**   Obviously you'd put more confidence in a site recommended, say, by NASCAR itself than by
one listed on Billy-Bob's Racin' Archives. That's not to say that
sites listed at Billy-Bob's are bad, but it's human nature to place
more confidence in a known entity.

- **Subject indexes**   Sometimes you're just in the mood to surf on
a certain subject. One of the best ways to start such an adventure
is to use a subject index. We'll discuss these more thoroughly
later in the lesson.

- **Searching for clues**   A well-thought-out search using an appropriate search engine can be incredibly fruitful when it comes to
homing in on something very specific. We'll cover search
engines in great detail later in this lesson.

Many of these methods are pretty self-explanatory, but the last two—
subject indexes and search engines—are worth exploring in detail. They
may seem like simple concepts on the surface, but there are some
subtleties that can help maximize your results while minimizing your
expenditure of time.

Staying On Topic: The Value of Subject Indexes

Have you ever finished a tasty meal with the feeling you'd love to have something sweet, only you weren't sure what you wanted? Experiencing the Internet can be kind of the same. Your pulse quickens as the modem crackles into activity. You check your email and then set out to do some free surfing (non-task-oriented surfing, that is).

You've been thinking about getting a new puppy but aren't sure what kind. You've heard great things about Golden Retrievers but aren't sure you want a dog that big. This sort of unfocused wandering is a perfect candidate for using a subject index.

What Is a Subject Index?

A subject index is basically a site that sorts Web sites into a variety of broad subject areas such as entertainment, sports, computers, and shopping. Those primary subject areas are then sorted into smaller subject areas. For instance, sports might be broken down into categories such as basketball, water sports, gymnastics, and motor sports. And finally, motor sports might contain categories such as NASCAR and drag racing.

This structure makes it easy for you to find topics of general interest, while making it convenient to drill down to more specific material as you desire.

Because humans most commonly generate subject indexes, you often stand a better chance of finding good content quicker. Why? Because information goes where it should be placed, not where some mathematical formula says it should go. (This will make more sense as you read about search engines and how they work.)

The premiere subject index, Yahoo!, started the subject index rage and even spawned books and magazines dedicated to Web surfing. To follow in Yahoo!'s successful footsteps, many search engines have created their own subject indexes in addition to their searching capabilities. These subject indexes usually contain links to sources positively reviewed by the host site's personnel and, in some cases, are based on surveys completed by the users.

There must be some misunderstanding Please don't misunderstand what I'm saying here about Yahoo!. While it was primarily a subject index in its infancy, it has evolved to so much more today—a rich tool for searching the newswires and other valuable sources of information.

Where Can I Find Some Subject Indexes?

Check these sites when you want to go surfing but aren't exactly sure what you're looking for. You'll find gobs of good sites each time you log on, no matter what you're in the mood for.

- Yahoo! at http://www.yahoo.com

- Nerdworld at http://www.nerdworld.com

- The Mining Company at http://home.miningco.com/index.htm (there is no www preceding its address)

- Excite Channels at http://www.excite.com

- Infoseek Web Directory at http://www.infoseek.com

- Sites from A2Z at http://a2z.lycos.com (again, no www)

Drill Down Through Yahoo!'s Subject Index

Point your Web browser to http://www.yahoo.com and follow these steps to see just how simple it is to home in on very specific information by using a subject index:

1. Click **Recreation and Sports**.

2. Choose **Hobbies**.

3. Click **Collecting**.

4. Choose **Toys@**. (Did you notice air sickness bags and aluminum foil balls on the list of choices? Some people....)

5. Select **Stuffed Toys**.

6. Select **Beanie Babies**.

What's the @ for following the Category Listing?
Frequently you will see Yahoo! category titles listed
with a @ as a suffix to the category. The @ simply
means the category is referenced elsewhere in
Yahoo!.

See how quickly you were able to find something very specific? And best of all, you didn't have to plow through tens of thousands of links as you would with a search engine.

The Least You Need to Know About Search Engines...

The phrase "search engine" may conjure up images of squeaky, dusty old machinery lurching into action in some isolated warehouse, but they're really nothing to be afraid of or intimidated by.

Search engines are software tools you can use to search Web pages, newsgroups, and so on. Don't worry, they don't squeak or pinch your fingers! They index their information by sending all kinds of creepy crawlers—worms, spiders, and the like—around the Web. They follow every link they can find, indexing every word along the way. This is what makes them so valuable. With a well-placed query, you can snatch an elusive piece of information in a heartbeat.

There are several kinds of search engines, which I will discuss in the sections to follow.

Just the Basics

Calling these search engines basic is a bit of an understatement. They can often search the Web, newsgroups, sound files, and even the newswires in some cases. What's more, they can usually report the results in a variety of formats, depending on your specific needs. Structured queries are getting easier to submit every day, with drop-down boxes that enable you to determine whether the search should be run on the words you type as a phrase only, on one word or the other, on both words in the same document, and so on.

Because the ways search engines accept data can vary, I strongly urge you to read their individual search instructions. The time you spend doing that will pay for itself many times over.

 You're not out of your league Many search engines offer advanced search options. Don't let the word *advanced* intimidate you here. In the vast majority of cases, it only means you can specify more fields for the search. The bottom line is that if you're looking for something very specific, advanced search options can single-handedly save you from having to weed through hundreds of useless, unrelated Web sites. Go for it.

So where can you find some of these robust search engines? Read on to find out.

HotBot at http://www.hotbot.com

This search engine allegedly has indexed every word of more than 54 million documents. You can search the Web or newsgroups and can search by date, media type, location of the site, and so on. There is now a subject index available on the site also.

Excite at http://www.excite.com

Running a close second in size to HotBot, this engine has two search options: Simple and Power. While Simple is fairly self explanatory, you'll be interested to know that the Power search enables you to sift through news and City.Net (a guide of events, attractions, and so on for most cities around the country) and lets you search its reviewed sites only.

AltaVista at `http://www.altavista.com`

With an estimated 31 million sites indexed, this engine is no slouch either. You can also search the full text of more than 14,000 newsgroups, which is pretty neat. Like Excite, AltaVista has some advanced search options you'll want to explore.

Infoseek at `http://www.infoseek.com`

This search engine also gives you access to a pretty nice subject index, as well as front page links to a number of basic resources such as phone books and maps.

Lycos at `http://www.lycos.com`

One of the earliest search engines, this site houses all kinds of fun stuff to browse. And check out their Lycos Pro search options, which let you determine how your search results are reported.

DejaNews at `http://www.dejanews.com`

This search engine's claim to fame used to be its ability to search newsgroups, but now it does so much more. You can find other people with similar interests and research what people are saying about certain products. And, by the time you read this, who knows what else it'll have up its sleeve?

This list is by no means exhaustive, but it's more than enough to give you a taste of the individual search engines on the Internet.

When 50 Million Pages Isn't Enough, Try a Meta-Search

If you want to kill several birds with one stone, you may want to consider using a meta-search engine. These powerful beasts can search and return results from multiple search engines at the same time. That's right, only one query to enter. Of course you lose some of the functionality found in some of the search engines' advanced features, so there's a tradeoff to be made.

In some cases, you can select which search engines are part of the meta-search, whereas others operate with a set of defaults. Typically, the meta-search engine grinds through each search engine until a certain amount of time elapses. It may get through all of the search engines, or it may barely make it through one. A lot depends on how long the meta-search gives itself and how bogged down the Internet is at the time of your search.

The way meta-search engines return results varies widely, so I've provided information on a few of the more common meta-search sites.

Debriefing at `http:/www.debriefing.com`
This engine searches Infoseek, Excite, AltaVista, Lycos, Web Crawler, and Yahoo!. Debriefing's results are ranked in order of relevance, and duplicate links are weeded out for you so everything appears on a single list. You can increase or decrease the amount of time Debriefing gives itself by using the advanced options.

DigiSearch at `http://www.digiway.com/digisearch`
Pick any of the 18 search engines available to perform your search. You can also specify how much time is spent on the search. While the results from each search engine are presented separately, DigiSearch does give you the ability to search newsgroups and assorted directories.

Dogpile at `http://www.dogpile.com`
Despite its less-than-pretty name, Dogpile does produce, well, a pile of results. Unlike the others, however, it gives you the ability to search the newswires—the very thing that got me started on this tool in the first place. While the results seem to be achieved quickly, they are not combined, which means the same link could easily come up under each engine.

Again, this is just a small sampling of what's available out there. If used to their fullest potential, meta-searches can be invaluable tools.

Searching for a Search Engine?
Have you ever had a boss who was so into meetings that he'd plan a meeting to plan another meeting? The concept of searching for a search engine must appear nearly as ridiculous.

The last type of search tool I'm going to present is something occasionally referred to as an all-in-one page. These all-in-one pages contain text boxes for dozens if not hundreds (or even thousands) of searchable databases. The only real advantages to these sites are

- You only have to type one URL to reach a variety of resources.

- You can often search far more specialized databases of information than you can with the other search tools.

- You can create a page just like it that is made up of your own favorite sources. Just follow the directions provided on each site's home page.

Next are some all-in-one sites that you'll want to check out.

CINet's Search.com at `http://www.search.com`
This well-organized site is your gateway to more than one hundred search engines, ranging from the old standards like Excite to recipe databases.

The Internet Sleuth at `http://www.isleuth.com`
With a whopping two thousand-plus search engines, you'll need that search engine to search for a search engine.

Searching Internet Explorer Style

Now that you're familiar with some of the basics of searching on the Internet, it's time to shift our focus to searching the Internet via Internet Explorer. You could just type in the URLs provided earlier, but I think there are some things you'll want to consider first.

Internet Explorer 5 gives you some innovative new ways to search the Internet. In the sections that follow, I'll present these new features and follow them with a few search tips that will come in handy, no matter what method you use.

Searching with the New Search Assistant

Once you get used to it, you'll grow to love searching with this new tool. It lets you check out each link returned by the search engine without the hassle of having to click the Back button all the time.

Follow these steps to give searching with the Search Assistant a test drive:

1. With Internet Explorer running and an active connection to the Internet, click the **Search** button on the standard button bar. The Search Assistant pane on the left side of the screen (see Figure 9.1) appears with your preferred search engine all ready to go to work.

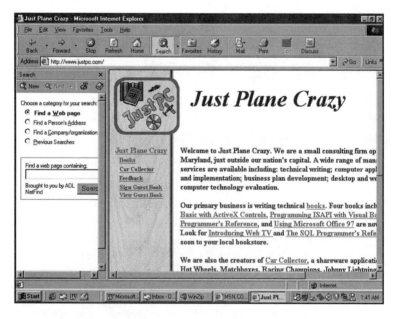

FIGURE 9.1 The Search Assistant pane lets you see your search results while you surf.

2. Don't like the search engine you see? Click the **Customize** button, second from the right edge at the top of the Search Assistant

pane. The page shown in Figure 9.2 appears, giving you a large selection from which to choose.

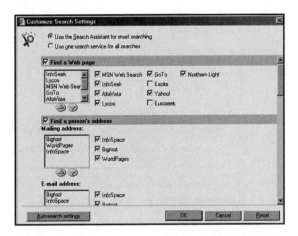

FIGURE 9.2   Place a check mark next to the provider(s) you want to use. Don't forget to scroll down the page; you have a lot of choices to make.

3. Place a check mark next to the search providers you want to use, and then click the OK button at the bottom of the screen.

4. Enter your word or phrase and perform the search as normal. The results will appear in the Search Assistant pane, as shown in Figure 9.3.

5. To view a link, simply click it. The page will be displayed in the main viewing window, as you saw in Figure 9.3.

6. When you want to switch to a new link, just click it—no more clicking the Back button 20 times in a single search.

7. When you're finished with the search, simply press the Search button on the standard button bar again. The Search Assistant will disappear, and your Internet Explorer screen will return to normal.

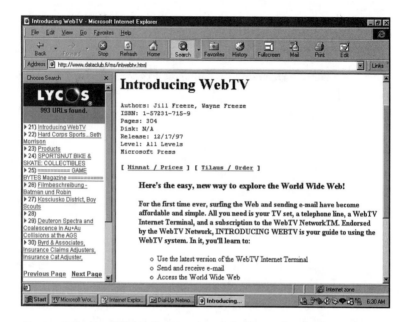

Figure 9.3   Just click a link to view it in the main viewing window.

Express Searching: When Only the Fastest Will Do

Internet Explorer 5's new AutoSearch feature lets you perform a search quickly from Internet Explorer's Address Bar. Say, for instance, you wanted to search on Calico Cat. In the Address Bar, type any of the following:

- ? calico cat

- go calico cat

- find calico cat

The links from which you can choose will appear in the main viewing area of Internet Explorer.

Is it too good to be true? Unfortunately, the new AutoSearch feature only supports one information provider—Yahoo!. While Yahoo! is a great site, it doesn't have the breadth and depth of a traditional search engine. But then again, it doesn't have all the clutter, either.

Finding Things on a Web Page

Some Web documents can ramble on forever, which is why you'll want to know how to perform a search on a specified Web page. Just follow these steps:

1. With the page you want to search displayed in Internet Explorer, press **Edit** on the menu bar and select **Find** (on this page). The dialog box shown in Figure 9.4 appears.

 A shortcut Instead of using the menu commands, you can press **Ctrl+F** to bring up the Find dialog box.

FIGURE 9.4   The Find dialog box helps you get where you want to go quickly.

2. Type in the word or phrase you wish to find on the current page.

3. Tell Internet Explorer whether you want it to look for a whole word match and whether you want it to match the case of the text you entered. Just place a check mark in the appropriate box(es).

4. Click the **Find Next** button to send Internet Explorer after the next occurrence of the word or phrase. You can even press the **Up** or **Down** button to tell Internet Explorer which way to go. (By the way, Down is the default.)

5. When you're finished with the search, click the **Close** button at the top-right side of the Find dialog box, or click **Cancel**. Either will remove the box from the screen.

You're a real Web warrior now! You should be able to home in on what you want in little or no time at all. In the next lesson, we'll venture into the world of email.

LESSON 10

Setting Up Outlook Express to Send and Receive Email

This lesson walks you through the setup and configuration of the newest version of Outlook Express.

Getting Outlook Express Ready to Receive Email

Microsoft may have made its software smart with wizards, agents, and such, but sometimes you still need to tell it what to do. (So Bill, when will the new version of Windows complete with the revolutionary psychic interface be released?)

Whether you're setting up an email program for the first time or you need to add your employer's email server to your Outlook Express configuration, you'll want to read the next section.

Adding an Email Server to Outlook Express

Launch Outlook Express by clicking the **Outlook Express** icon on your Windows desktop (or by selecting **Programs, Outlook Express** from the **Start** menu), and then follow these directions:

1. Click the Outlook Express **Tools** menu and select **Accounts**. Verify that the **Mail** tab is the one that's active. The Internet Accounts window appears (see Figure 10.1).

Click here and select Mail.

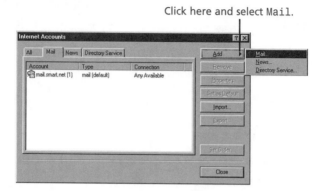

FIGURE 10.1   The Add button lets you choose the kind of account with which you want to work.

2. Click the **Add** button and select **Mail** from the list. The Internet Connection Wizard launches (see Figure 10.2).

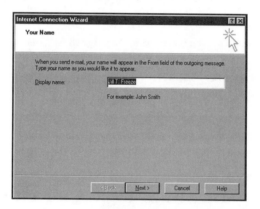

FIGURE 10.2   The Internet Connection Wizard leads you every step of the way.

3. The first screen asks you to enter your name as you want it to appear in the From field of your outgoing email messages. Type it in, and then click **Next**.

4. Next, you are asked to provide the email address assigned to you by your Internet service provider. At this point you can also opt

to set up your own Hotmail account, which will let you check your email from remote locations. Click Next when you are finished.

5. The next screen asks you to define what type of incoming mail server you have—POP3 or IMAP. Use the drop-down arrow to make your selection. If you're not sure of your selection here, don't be afraid to ask your Internet service provider (ISP). Then you must type in the names of both the incoming and outgoing mail servers before clicking Next.

IMAP (Internet Message Access Protocol)   The latest and greatest protocol available for retrieving email messages, IMAP allows you to organize messages on your mail server into folders. You can also store sent mail and drafts on your server for access from various locations. Outlook Express supports IMAP. However, not all Internet service providers offer IMAP support. POP3 (short for Post Office Protocol 3), on the other hand, stores all the messages on the mail server until you log on, at which point all of the messages are automatically downloaded to your machine. However, many POP3 email programs now have options to keep messages on the server.

IMAP—it's not just for business people anymore! That's right, casual users can also benefit from IMAP's many features. With continually falling PC prices, many households now have multiple PCs. With POP3, messages retrieved on one machine stay there (unless you've specifically set an option to the contrary), which means someone checking mail from another machine can miss an important message entirely. IMAP, however, leaves the messages on the mail server until you explicitly download them. This enables you to check your email from literally anywhere.

6. Your Internet logon information is requested in this screen, namely your account name/user ID and password. Once they've been entered, click Next to continue.

7. Next, you are asked to tell the wizard what type of connection you want to establish. Connect Using My Phone Line is the most common option. Click Next to continue.

8. Select which modem you'll use to connect to the account, and then click Next.

9. This screen asks which dial-up connection you want to use to access the mail server. Most likely you'll choose from an existing one. Click Next.

10. It's time to celebrate; you've entered all the information needed. All you have to do is close the Accounts dialog box and then click Finish.

Now Outlook Express will know where to look for incoming mail and where to route outgoing messages.

Take a deep breath, you made it. In fact, if this is your first email account, you're all done with the setup stuff. If, on the other hand, you're migrating to Outlook Express from a different mail program, you've got one last thing to do.

 Migrating Yes, I realize email messages are not birds flocking to the south to escape a cold, hard winter. People in the computer business often refer to the act of moving from one program to another similar program as *migrating*.

Migrating to Outlook Express

With the newest version of Outlook Express, it's even easier to make the big switch from other popular programs, such as Netscape Communicator, Microsoft Exchange, Eudora Pro or Light (up through version 3.0), or previous releases of Outlook Express. And if Microsoft repeats history, it'll

probably come out with even more import capabilities as time goes on, so
keep an eye on Microsoft's Outlook Express Web site.

Importing Email Messages into Outlook Express

Follow these steps carefully to bring messages from other programs into
Outlook Express:

1. With Outlook Express running, click the **Inbox** icon in the
   Folder List, as shown in Figure 10.3.

Click here to begin.

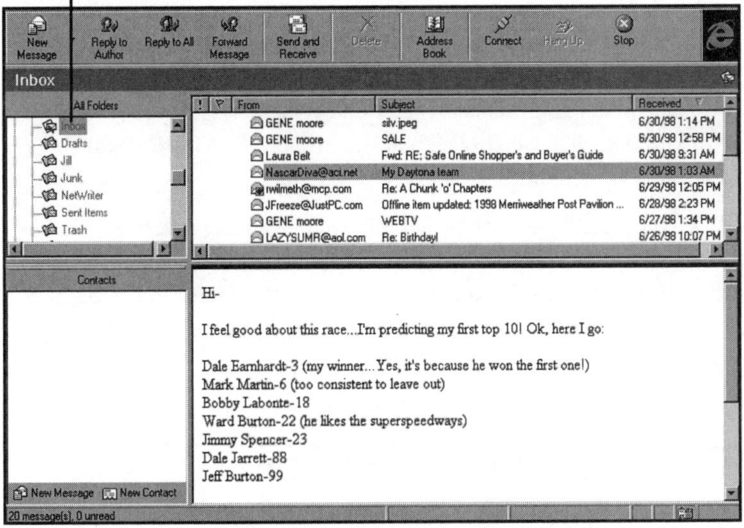

Figure 10.3 Click the **Inbox** icon to start the importing process.

2. On the **File** menu, choose **Import, Messages**. Guess what pops
   up—another wizard, called the Outlook Express Import Wizard.

3. The opening screen, shown in Figure 10.4, asks from which
   email program you'd like to import messages. Select the appropriate choice, and then press **Next**.

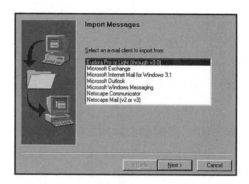

Figure 10.4   Meet the Outlook Express Import Wizard.

4. The wizard snoops around your computer's hard drive in search of the messages. When it finds the location in which the messages are stored, it displays the filename and asks you to verify it. If the wizard cannot readily find your messages, you may need to click the **Browse** button and show the wizard where they're stored. Click **Next** when finished.

5. The wizard may or may not ask you a few more questions before the import is complete; it depends on the program from which you're importing the messages. The wizard won't lead you astray. Just follow its lead, clicking **Next** and **Finish** as directed.

Changing the Sound that Plays when New Mail Comes

Unless you tell it otherwise, Outlook Express will emit what can best be described as a ding-like sound when new messages arrive. (Microsoft refers to the sound as chimes, though I beg to differ.) If you want to get creative and try something a bit more unique, follow these steps:

1. Click the **Start** button on the Windows taskbar, and then select **Settings, Control Panel.**

2. Double-click (or click if using the Active Desktop) the **Sounds** icon. The Sounds Properties dialog box appears (see Figure 10.5).

FIGURE 10.5   While this is really a Windows setting, it is of value to the Outlook Express user as well.

3. Click the **New Mail Notification** item to select it.

4. Use the drop-down arrow next to the Sound Name box to choose a new sound. You can preview the sound by choosing the **Play** button in the Preview section of the dialog box.

.WAV **to your email!**   The New Mail Notification sound event can be virtually any .wav file you may already have on your system (or one you track down on the Internet, for that matter). To select a .wav file, click the **Browse** button and click your way to the desired filename on your machine.

5. After you've found a sound you like, click **Apply** to define the setting, and then click **OK** to save the setting and close the dialog box.

In this lesson, you learned how to set Outlook Express up as your mail server, so you should be ready to dive right in now. In the next lesson, I cover sending email messages using Outlook Express.

LESSON 11

Sending Email with Outlook Express

This lesson walks you through the setup and configuration of the newest version of Outlook Express.

The Anatomy of the Outlook Express Workspace

You've got to send email to receive email, that's just sort of the way it works. (Well, except for that pesky virtual junk mail, but that's another story…). Of course, before you can do anything with Outlook Express, you'll need to learn your way around the workspace. What are the various screen elements called? What kinds of things will you see there? These are all critical bits of information you'll need to make the most of this book as well as Microsoft's help files. Figure 11.1 illustrates a sample Outlook Express screen.

The title bar, menu bar, and Outlook toolbar (or button bar) are nearly identical to ones you'll find in other Windows applications. The title bar presents the name of the application along with the currently selected element, and the menu and button bars are tweaked slightly to include functions needed for Outlook Express's messaging capabilities. Table 11.1 describes elements unique to Outlook Express and how they function.

Folder Bar   Folder List
Title Bar   Menu Bar   Outlook Toolbar   Inbox   Mail/News
                                                         Column Headers

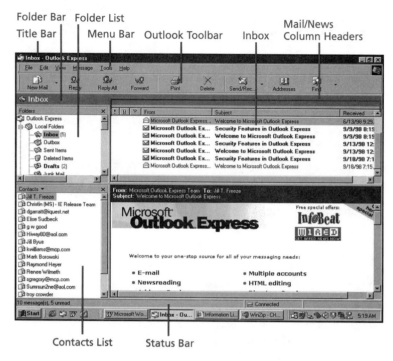

Contacts List   Status Bar

FIGURE 11.1 Outlook Express screen elements.

TABLE 11.1 Descriptions of Outlook Express-Specific Elements

Element	Function
Folder Bar	Displays the name of the currently selected folder.
Folder List	Holds the folders you've defined in Outlook Express, including ones for your mail and news server.
Inbox	Lists all messages contained in the currently selected folder.
Contacts List	If you have a meager- size Contacts list like I do, you can see nearly every entry in the Contacts List pane.

Element	Function
Status Bar	Tells you how much of the selected message or file has been downloaded.
Mail/News Column Headers	Labels each of the displayed elements in the currently selected folder.

Now that you've got your bearings, let's zoom in on the toolbar buttons you'll use in Outlook Express (see Figure 11.2).

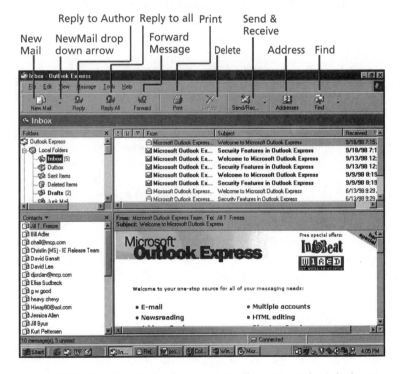

FIGURE 11.2 Use the Outlook Express toolbar to get the job done quickly.

They are, from left to right, as follows:

- **New Mail**—Click this button to start composing a new email message or to post an article in a newsgroup.

- **New Mail Drop-down Arrow**—Click this button to compose a new message with one of the pieces of stationery supplied with Outlook Express.

- **Reply to Author**—By clicking this button with a message selected and/or displayed, you send a reply to that message to the author only, not everyone else who may have received the message.

- **Reply to All**—Use this button with the desired message displayed or selected to respond to everyone to whom the message was originally sent.

You never know who may be listening... Use extreme caution when choosing Reply to All. An email address may often contain few clues as to who is actually going to receive a message. For example, your boss's personal email address might be something like CelticFan@JustPC.com. You wouldn't want anything incriminating to get into his hands, so, unless you're absolutely sure who will be reading the message, I suggest you stick with the Reply to Author button.

- **Forward Message**—Want to share an email message with someone else? Select it, and then select the Forward Message button.

- **Print**—If you need a hard copy of a piece of email, this is the place to click.

- **Delete**—Use this button to delete the currently selected message. Note that the message will just be crossed out and tagged until you deliberately purge it.

- **Send and Receive**—This button, which sends and checks your mail while connected to the mail server, opens up a status window that reports the status of tasks currently being handled by Outlook Express. It also reports on any errors it encounters.

- **Addresses**—Click Addresses if you want to look up, add, or edit a contact in your Address Book.

Composing an Email Message

For your email message to reach its destination, you'll need to have the recipient's email address. This address is commonly expressed in the format *personsname@adomain.com*. Any address not conforming to the proper format will result in the message being returned to the sender.

 Domain The name given to a computer that is an officially registered provider of information on the Internet. Domain names are usually made up of two or more elements separated by periods. Some examples are msn.com, webtv.net, umass.edu, and justpc.com.

Sending a Message to One Recipient

To send a message to another person on the Internet, follow these simple steps:

1. With Outlook Express up and running, click the New Mail button. A New Message window appears (see Figure 11.3).

2. The insertion point blinks in the To: field, prompting you to enter the desired email address. Type in the address, verifying that it conforms to the standard email address format. You can also select an address from your Address book, which I'll cover in more detail in Lesson 13, "Setting up Your Address Book."

3. Next, click the Subject: line area and enter a descriptive title for the message.

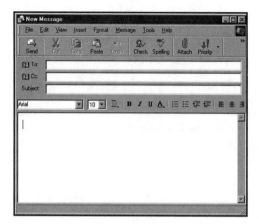

FIGURE 11.3 The New Message screen is where it all begins, whether you're sending a note to one person or many people.

 Not to change the subject or anything... Try to make the subject lines of your messages as succinct as possible, while making sure the true essence of the message is spelled out. How can you tell if you've accomplished this? Ask yourself the following: Will the recipient be able to assess the urgency of the contents based on the subject line? Will he or she likely know what you're referring to in the subject line? An affirmative answer to either of these means you're off to a good start.

4. Click inside the main pane of the New Message window, which is where you'll write the body of your message.

5. When you've finished typing your message, click the Send button on the far left of the message toolbar to send it on its way.

How fast is fast? If you don't believe email is a fast method of communication, try this little experiment: Compose a new message and place the following address in the To: line: **Netwriter@JustPC.com**. Type **IE 5 Test** in the Subject line, and then click the Send button. Wait a few seconds, and then press the F5 key to refresh your inbox. Barring a major Internet traffic jam, you should see a response from the Netwriter autoreply I've set up.

Can you believe it? A message traveled to my mail server in Maryland and back to you that quickly. I don't care if you live across the street or halfway around the globe, that's pretty amazing!

Sending a Message to Multiple Recipients

There are a variety of ways in which you can send a message to multiple people, and each method means something slightly different.

You can include multiple email addresses in the To: line; just separate them with a comma (,) or semicolon (;). This method is best used in instances where every addressee is a targeted recipient of the message. For example if you manage a group of people, you may want to notify all of them when you'll be out of the office on vacation. In this case, each person is the intended recipient of the message.

Let Outlook do the work for you! You may also simply press the Enter key to enter the separating commas.

You can also use the CC: (carbon copy) line for multiple recipients. This differs from the method previously described in that addressees defined on the CC: line are not expected to take action on the message. If, for example, you need to send an important note to a client, you may want to send your boss a copy of the note for his information. This is the perfect time to use the CC: line. And, if you need to, you can include multiple addresses on the CC: line simply by separating them with a comma or semicolon.

Finally, there's the BCC: (blind carbon copy) line. Placing addresses in this line makes them invisible to the primary recipient of the message. You may want to use BCC: when emailing a staff member about potential disciplinary action so your boss has a copy for her information. This may help you down the road should the situation turn ugly.

Creating the Message Body

You may think there's little more to composing a message than just plain typing. Well, you're only half right. Yes, it can be that simple, but you can do so much more with formatting messages in Outlook Express. You can generate a bulleted list; use flashy stationery; add a unique signature, and so on.

It all begins with Outlook Express's counterpart to the Standard toolbar—the Message toolbar (see Figure 11.4). If you've used any other Microsoft applications, you'll undoubtedly recognize some of the buttons and their functions.

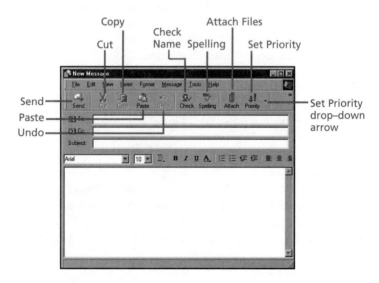

FIGURE 11.4 These buttons handle your basic text manipulation.

- **Send**—Click this button to send your message on its way when you've finished writing.

- **Cut**—Want to move a block of text somewhere else in your message? Just select it using your mouse, and then click the Cut button. The text will disappear and be held in a virtual clipboard until you paste it in the desired location.

- **Copy**—Select text you want to have repeated elsewhere in the message (or in another message for that matter), and then click the Copy button. The text will remain in its original location as well as in the clipboard for later use.

- **Paste**—Use this button to place text stored in your clipboard in the desired position.

- **Undo**—If you need to undo the last formatting change you made, use this button. If works for deleting text, too, but is slower than using other methods like the Backspace button, the Delete button, or highlighting the desired text and pressing Delete.

- **Check Names**—Can you only remember part of an email address? After you've typed in the portion you know, click the Check Names button. Outlook Express will search your Address Book for a match. If it finds more than one, it will list them all, so you can pick the one you want.

- **Spelling**—Use this tool to check your email for spelling errors prior to sending it.

- **Attach**—Click this button to attach a file—such as a Word document or scanned photo—to the current email message. That way, if the recipient has the proper software, he or she can view the attachment and work with it as well.

- **Set Priority**—If you need to draw attention to a message, this is the way to do it. Choose this button to cycle through your options. These are Normal (default), High, and Low priority (see Figure 11.5).

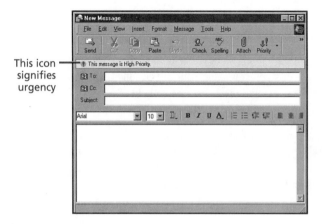

This icon signifies urgency

Figure 11.5 The icon shown here tells you at what priority level the current message is set.

- **Set Priority Dropdown Arrow**—You can also set a message's priority by clicking the **Set Priority** arrow and dragging the mouse pointer to the desired priority level.

The toolbar immediately above the composition window—the Formatting toolbar—gives you all kinds of tools to help you format your message and make it look nice. It's identical to Word's Formatting toolbar, so you should have no difficulty creating the text effects you desire.

Attaching a File to Your Message

On occasion, you may have the desire (or need) to attach a file to a message. Perhaps it's a Microsoft Word file with a favorite recipe or a recently scanned photo of your new home. There are countless reasons why you may want to attach a file to your message, and the best news of all is it's an easy thing to do. Just follow these steps:

1. With the message displayed onscreen, simply click the **Attach** button on the toolbar. You'll see a dialog box nearly identical to the typical Open or Save dialog box (see Figure 11.6).

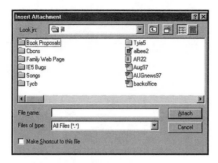

Figure 11.6 Click your way to the file you want to attach.

2. Click your way through the directories until you see the file you want to attach.

3. When you've found the file, click it to select it, and then click **Attach**. You will see a new line under the Subject line of your message called Attach, which displays the filename and size. And the paper clip icon will appear next to the Internet Explorer icon to let you know that the file was successfully attached.

In this lesson, you familiarized yourself with the Outlook Express workspace and learned how to send messages. With that mastered, you'll want to learn how to do the fancy and fun stuff like creating personal stationery and using signature files. I'll show you how in Lesson 12.

LESSON 12

Advanced Outlook Express Mail Sending Options

This lesson shows you how to add some life to your Outlook Express messages.

Working with Outlook Express Stationery

Do you wish there were an electronic counterpart to all that fancy stationery you used to write letters as a child? You're in luck; Outlook Express stationery fits the bill. It's graphically appealing, it doesn't shift the focus from the words to the artwork and, best of all, it's easy to implement (see Figure 12.1) and easy to view, provided the recipient uses an email client capable of reading HTML.

In the latest version of Outlook Express, you have a variety of themes to choose from, including baby news, birthday balloons, Christmas trees, and for sale.

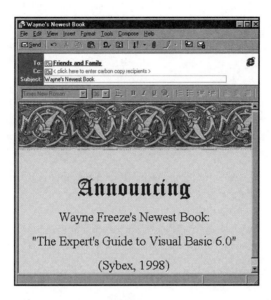

FIGURE 12.1 Choose from a variety of neat themed stationery included with Outlook Express, such as this formal announcement.

Composing a Message with Outlook Express Stationery

You'll need to follow these steps to begin composing a message with Outlook Express stationery:

1. With Outlook Express up and running, click the arrow next to the New Mail button. Roll your mouse pointer down the list until you see the stationery you want to use, or click Select Stationery to see additional choices.

2. If you opt to see more choices, you'll see a dialog box like the one shown in Figure 12.2. Click a filename to see a preview of it in the Preview window at the right end of the dialog box.

FIGURE 12.2 The Select Stationery dialog box lets you preview your options before you select.

3. If the preview meets with your approval, click OK. A New Message window using the stationery you selected pops up.

4. Enter the email address, subject line, and message as usual, and then send it off.

To apply stationery after a message has been written, click Format, and then select Apply Stationery.

Building a Signature File

Because you can't sign your email with a pen in a personalized fashion, you must turn to alternate ways to label a message as yours. With email, this is typically done using signature files. To begin building a signature file, you'll need to follow these steps:

1. Have Outlook Express up and running, but you needn't be connected to the Internet.

2. On the Outlook Express menu bar, click Tools, and then select Options.

3. Click the Signatures tab to display the dialog box shown in Figure 12.3.

FIGURE 12.3 The Signatures tab is where you'll begin designing your signature files.

4. Click the New button to begin. The words "Signature #1" will appear lightly highlighted in the Signatures box. This acts as the new signature's temporary name. Also notice that the insertion point is blinking in the text box below.

5. Type in your signature text, which can be as simple as your name and email address only, or as complex as an intricate piece of ASCII art (letters and symbols combined to make a larger picture).

6. When you're satisfied with the text that's in place, click the Rename button to give the signature a unique name. Signature #1 will be highlighted, so all you have to do is begin typing the name you want to use.

Appropriately enough... Be sure the name you assign is short and clearly defines the contents, because you'll be accessing the .sig file from a drop-down menu that doesn't have hoards of space in which to display names.

7. Once you've created all of the signature files you want (you can easily return at a later date, so there's no rush to do it all up front), select the **Apply** button to save your additions.

8. Click **OK** to close the dialog box and continue working in Outlook Express.

Setting a Default Signature

Outlook Express labels the first signature file you create as the default signature. If you're anything like me, the first signature file you built was probably a fun one, so you may need to redefine the default.

 Decisions, decisions... Before specifying your default signature, think about which one you're likely to use most. In your situation, the fun one may very well be the best choice.

If different signatures are so easy to apply, why should you bother defining the default? Because, as you will see in subsequent sections, it's nearly effortless to attach the default signature to a message. Furthermore, Outlook Express will use the default signature any time you tell it to include a signature on outgoing messages.

Here's what you'll need to do to tell Outlook Express which signature you want to use as your default:

1. Launch Outlook Express (no connection to the Internet needed), and access the **Signatures** tab of the **Options** menu as described in the previous section.

2. Click the signature you want to use as the default to mark it.

3. Click the **Set as Default** button. Notice the words "Default Signature" appear next to the name of the signature you chose.

4. If you approve of the settings, click **Apply** to save them.

5. Finally, click **OK** to close the dialog box and continue working with Outlook Express.

Telling Outlook Express Which Signature to Use When

This feature is one of those "good news, bad news" things. You get really revved up about what it can potentially do, but you discover it falls just short of what you wish it could do.

With this release of Outlook Express, you can assign a different signature to each news server and mail server you use. Neat, huh? Well this is where you start wishing it could go one step further. I'd love to be able to define a particular signature for each newsgroup to which I subscribe. Unfortunately, it'll have to wait for now. At least multiple signature support is a big step in the right direction.

Follow these steps to tell Outlook Express which signature to use with each news/mail server:

1. Access the **Signatures** tab from within Outlook Express as described earlier.

2. Click a signature you'd like to use for either email or news posts.

3. Click the **Advanced** button. The dialog box shown in Figure 12.4 appears.

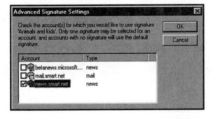

FIGURE 12.4 In the Advanced Signature Settings box, you can choose the category of messages to which you'd like the current signature to apply.

4. Place a check mark in the box next to the type of messages you'd like to have use the chosen signature.

Clearing up muddy waters You can use a single signature for more than one type of message, but you cannot use more than one signature for each type of message. In situations where the signature you chose is inappropriate, you'll have to delete the signature and insert a new one manually, as instructed in the following section.

5. Click **OK** to confirm your selection. You will return to the Signatures tab.

Twice the trouble If you assign a certain signature to a specific message type and then later inadvertently assign another signature to the same message type, Outlook Express will throw out your first choice in favor of the current one.

6. Repeat these steps as many times as necessary.

When in doubt, use the default If you don't specify a certain signature for use with a given message type, Outlook Express will use the default signature.

7. Verify that Add Signatures to All Outgoing Messages is checked. At this point, you can also tell Outlook Express whether or not to attach signatures to message replies and forwards by checking the Don't Add Signatures to Replies and Forwards box.

8. Click **Apply**, and then click **OK** to close the dialog box.

Applying a Signature to an Outgoing Message

Say you've decided not to have Outlook Express automatically apply a signature to every outgoing message. That doesn't mean you can't add one on-the-fly if you want.

To append the signature you designated as the default to the current message, just click the **Signature** button as shown in Figure 12.5.

Click here to add the default signature.

FIGURE 12.5 Click the Signature button to append the default signature to the current message.

If you want to add one of the other signatures you have tucked away, click the drop-down arrow next to the Signature button, and roll your mouse pointer down to the desired signature title. Now you know why I wanted you to use short but descriptive names for your signatures.

Spell Checking Your Messages

Few things drive me crazier than seeing spelling errors in professional documents. Thanks to Outlook Express's spell checker, you are able to avoid a number of embarrassing spelling errors.

To fire off the spell checker, click **Tools**, and select **Spelling**. The Spelling dialog box shown in Figure 12.6 appears. Use Table 12.1 as a guide for how to deal with errors tagged by the spell checker.

FIGURE 12.6 You can take a variety of actions on tagged errors.

TABLE 12.1 Actions to Be Taken in the Spelling Dialog Box

To do this...	...Do this
Change the word tagged to one not suggested	Type the new word in the Change To box, and then click the **Change** button. Use the **Change All** button instead if you need to make the change in multiple locations.
Change the word tagged to one suggested by the spell checker	Click the suggestion you want to accept, and then click the **Change** button or the **Change All** button if the word appears in multiple locations in the message.

To do this...	...Do this
Add the word to your dictionary so it won't be tagged again in the future (great for people's names)	Click the **Add** button.
Ignore the tagged word (good for acronyms, proper names, and such)	Use **Ignore** for single instances of the word or **Ignore All** for multiple occurrences of the word.
Cancel the change you just requested	Click **Cancel**.
Undo the previous change	Click **Undo Last**.

With the knowledge gained in this lesson, you'll be turning out fancy messages like a pro! But there's even more you can do—you can include a sound file, put your favorite image in with the text, change the color of the message's background, and so on.

In the next lesson, I'll show you how to set up your Address Book so you can save time and get organized all at once.

LESSON 13

Setting Up Your Address Book

This lesson helps you get organized and simplifies sending email messages by making use of the Address Book.

Adding Information to Your Address Book

Before you can do much of anything with your Address Book, you'll need to enter some data. To begin filling your book with all kinds of useful tidbits, follow these steps:

1. With Outlook Express up and running, click the **Addresses** button on the standard toolbar. A window displaying a list of previously defined contacts appears. If this is the first time you've selected the Addresses button and you filled out the information for the Profile Assistant covered earlier in the book, your information will be displayed. If not, the fields will be empty.

2. Click the **New** button at the top of the page and select **New Contact**. A window like the one shown in Figure 13.1 appears.

   In the Name tab, you'll have the opportunity to enter the following information:

   - **Name** Includes separate fields for first, middle, last name, a Display field for the name as it will appear on your Contacts List (automatically taken from the three name fields), and an optional Nickname field in which you can place the person's screen name or nickname.

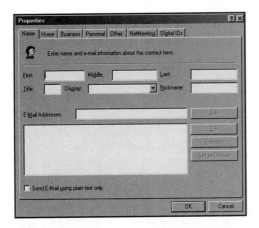

FIGURE 13.1 The Name tab asks for basic information about the contact.

- **E-Mail Addresses** Type in the contact's email address and then click the Add button. This first address will automatically be declared the person's default email address. You can add additional email addresses by typing them in and clicking the Add button.

3. Enter all known information about the contact on this first tab, including a nickname if you have one you'd like to use.

4. Click the Home tab to insert personal information about the contact, including the address of his or her personal home page if one exists (see Figure 13.2).

The Home tab gives you places to insert the following information:

- Street Address
- City
- State/Province
- Zip Code
- Country
- Phone
- Fax
- Cellular Phone Number

- Gender
- Personal Web Page Address

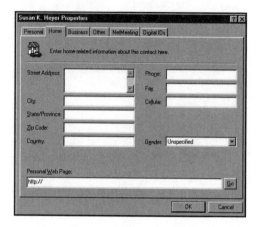

FIGURE 13.2 The Home tab lets you keep track of a contact's home address, phone number, and so on.

5. To enter information about your contact's place of employment, click the **Business** tab. You'll have spots to enter the job title, the department he or she works in, Fax number, pager number, and so on, as indicated by the presence of the following fields:

- Company
- Street Address
- City
- State/Province
- Zip Code
- Country
- Job Title
- Department
- Office
- Phone
- Fax
- Pager
- Business Web Page Address

6. Click the **Personal** tab to track additional information about a contact, such as birthday, spouse's/children's names, and so on.

7. The Other tab lets you enter any information that falls outside the categories provided. For example, you might want to include notes about where you met, what acquaintances you share, and so on.

8. When you've finished entering all of the data you can find, click the **OK** button. The contact information will be saved in your Address Book.

 The least you'll need... You don't have to fill in all of the fields to generate the address book entry. All you really need is the person's name and email address. If you have more information, great. If you don't, you needn't worry about Outlook Express aborting the entry due to lack of information.

Automatically Add Contacts to Your Address Book

With Outlook Express, it's possible to add contact information to your Address Book automatically. However, that information will only include the contact's name (if defined in his or her email program's From: line) and email address. If you want more, you'll have to flesh it out later; but at least the basic contact will have been generated for you.

To have Outlook Express automatically add contact information, do the following:

1. Launch Outlook Express as usual.

2. On the menu bar, click **Tools**, and then select **Options**. Click **Send** to open the tab illustrated in Figure 13.3.

3. Make sure there's a check in the Automatically Put People I Reply to in My Address Book check box.

4. Click the **Apply** button if necessary. (You won't need to click it if the box was already checked when you entered the menu.)

5. Click **OK** to exit the Options menu.

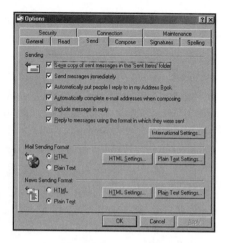

FIGURE 13.3 The Send tab of the Options dialog box is where you'll tell Outlook Express to automatically save contact information.

Composing a New Message Using Address Book Information

If you hate having to memorize (let alone type) lengthy email addresses, you'll love using your Outlook Express Address Book. There are multiple ways to retrieve a contact's email address from your Address Book when composing a new message.

To launch a new message box with a single recipient's email address already included, double-click the desired person's contact icon in the Contacts List pane. If your needs are a bit more complex, do any of the following:

- Click the **New Mail** button as usual, and then click the contact icon in the To: line to launch the Select Recipients dialog box shown in Figure 13.4. If you've already got the primary recipient's address in place, click the contact icon in the CC: line and proceed to the next step.

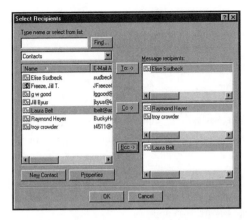

FIGURE 13.4 The Select Recipients dialog box makes it easy to put the contacts you want in the place you want them.

- With the New Message dialog box displayed, select the **To:** (or **CC:** or **BCC:**, as appropriate) button on the window's header section. See instructions for working with this dialog box in the next section.

- Begin typing the person's real name in the To: line or the CC: line. Outlook Express will use AutoComplete to "guess" the desired contact's name. If the name that appears looks like it matches the one you have in mind, click the **Check Names** button to have Outlook Express retrieve the corresponding email address from the contact file. Once the contact's email address has been successfully linked with the name, the name will appear in an underlined font. You're ready to compose your message and send it.

Working with the Select Recipients Dialog Box

If you chose a method that led you to the Select Recipients dialog box, you'll be relieved to find how simple it is to use. Basically, all you have to do is click the desired contact's name, click the button that corresponds to the message line on which you want the recipient's address to appear, repeat as needed, and then click **OK** to set the addresses in place. You're ready to go.

Editing a Contact's Information

People are constantly moving, changing jobs, or whatever. As a result, you'll want to know how to change the data contained in your Address Book. It's really quite simple, as you will see in the following steps

1. With Outlook Express up an running (no Internet connection needed), select the **Addresses** button on the toolbar. The screen shown in Figure 13.5 appears.

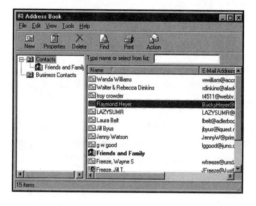

FIGURE **13.5** The Address Book screen gives you a good, at-a-glance view of your contacts.

2. Use the scrollbars to move to the desired contact. If you have a huge list, you can type the name into the Type Name box. As you type each letter, Outlook Express will highlight the closest match.

3. Once you've found the entry you need to modify, double-click it. The familiar Properties dialog box corresponding to the selected contact will open.

4. To edit an element, select the appropriate tab on the Summary screen and then just click inside the desired field's text box and make the necessary changes. Don't forget to visit each of the tabs that may be affected by the change(s).

5. When all the necessary changes have been made, click **OK** to save them.

In this lesson, you got your Address Book up and running. Now you shouldn't have any trouble locating the email addresses of your friends and associates when you need them. In the next lesson, we finally get into the nitty-gritty of reading email.

LESSON 14
Reading Email

This lesson teaches you all of the subtle nuances of reading email messages using Outlook Express.

Assessing What You've Got

Before we go any further, we need to establish what kind of email server you're running on—POP3 or IMAP. While it may not seem like a big deal in the scheme of things, you should know that Outlook Express behaves differently, depending on the type of mail server you're using.

When you log on to your Internet service provider and launch Outlook Express, the mail you've received appears in the Message List box, often called the Inbox. Several items are displayed by default for each piece of mail (see Figure 14.1); they include the following:

- **Priority** The first column is the Priority column. Look here to see which messages are high and low-level priorities. If a message carries a high priority level, a red exclamation point appears. If it's low level, a blue down-arrow will appear. Finally, if this column is blank, it means the message carries the default normal priority level.

- **Attachment** Presents a paper clip icon to tell you whether or not a file attachment is present in a given message.

- **Flag** Click inside this column to flag a message for future action. A little red flag icon appears to remind you that you need to revisit the message.

- **Mark for Retrieval** People accessing an IMAP mail server can leave all their messages on the server and check the ones they want to download by clicking this column.

- **From** This column displays the name or email address of the person or company sending the email message.

Attachment   Mark for Retrieval (IMAP servers only)

Priority   Flag   From   Subject   Received

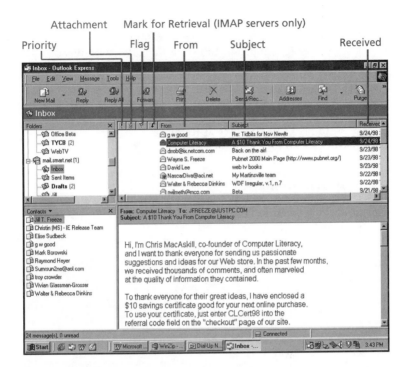

FIGURE 14.1 Use this information to determine what a message is about before you open it.

Who? Can't see the full name of a message's sender? Just run your mouse over the line in question. A screen tip–like box displaying the full content of the line appears. This trick works for long subject lines as well.

- **Subject** Hopefully this column provides a vivid description of the message content so you know where to place it in your personal priority list. Of course, the subject title's accuracy relies entirely on the sender, so you'll need to judge it accordingly.

- **Received** This bit of information tells you when the given message appeared in your mailbox.

Hey, who took my mail? If you configured your Internet connection to take advantage of IMAP support, you'll see two Inboxes: one under Outlook Express that will remain empty, and one under the name of your IMAP server that will hold all of your messages. Sound confusing? It can be, but I'll attempt to clarify all that in this lesson.

Reading a Message

When you click a message, its contents will appear in the Preview pane (see Figure 14.2).

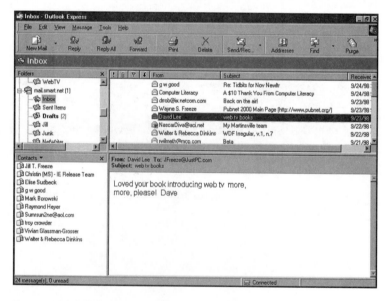

FIGURE 14.2 Click a message to see it in the Preview pane.

If you want to work with a copy of the message in its own message window, double-click it. When you're finished reading, click the **Close** button to close the message window.

New messages will appear in boldface type with a closed envelope icon. Once you've read a message, the envelope icon will appear to be opened (see Figure 14.3). And if you use an IMAP server, you'll see a partial envelope icon that means the message is on the server, but hasn't been downloaded to your machine yet.

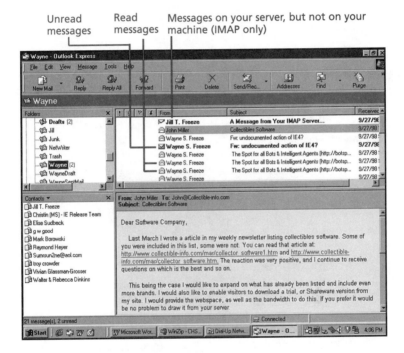

FIGURE 14.3 Outlook Express makes it easy to see which messages you have and haven't read.

Reading File Attachments

When you double-click a message to read its contents, there are three ways you can tell if the message contains an attached file (actually four, if you count the obnoxiously long download times of messages with long attachments):

- If the Attachment column appears on your Message List display, you'll see a paper clip icon on the line of messages containing an attachment.

- If a file attachment is present, a paper clip icon will appear next to the Internet Explorer icon at the top-right corner of the message window. You must have double-clicked the message to see this.

- Look for the Attach line underneath the Subject line. In it, you'll see an icon representing the file type of the attachment, and you'll see the name and size of the file.

To open the attached file, double-click its icon in the Attach line of the message. An Open Attachment Warning box like the one shown in Figure 14.4 appears. Click **Open It** to have Outlook Express automatically launch the necessary helper application (if one that can handle the file resides on your machine) or **Save It to Disk** to choose a home for the attachment on your machine.

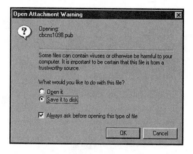

FIGURE **14.4** You can open the attachment on the spot or save it in an easy-to-remember location on your computer.

 Helper application In this context, it means the program needed to view the attached file.

Put on the brakes! If the attached file contains an `.exe` or `.com` file extension, do not open it until you've verified the sender of the file. Even opening a Word document or Excel spreadsheet can be potentially dangerous if the sender has incorporated a malicious macro. Opening such a file can potentially unleash a harmful virus if the source is not trustworthy.

 You can never be too cautious Be sure to install and run an antivirus program on your machine at all times for further protection. And remember to keep updating the antivirus program as well, since it can only "cure" viruses with which it knows how to deal.

Taking Action on a Message

Once you receive a message, there are a variety of actions you can take on them, ranging from deleting them to replying to them to saving them. In the following sections, you'll see just how simple it is to perform each action.

Deleting a Message

As time goes on, you'll get more junk mail than you know what to do with. That's why you'll want—and need—to know every possible way to delete a message.

When you glance at your Message List, you can tell some items are junk mail at the get-go because you won't recognize the From address, or the subject line will read something like "Make $10,000 in a week!" To delete these, all you have to do is click the message to mark it and then press the **Delete** button.

So you hate taking out the trash, huh? There's good news and bad news. The good news is you can have Outlook Express do it automatically. The bad news is if you do it this way, there's no turning back once you shut down Outlook Express—the messages are gone for good. You be the judge, but don't say I didn't warn you. Proceed with caution.

If you really want to have Outlook Express perform this task, do the following: Open the Tools menu and select Options. On the Maintenance tab, place a check mark next to the first item, which reads Empty Messages from the Deleted Items Folder on Exit. Click Apply and then OK, and you're good to go.

On POP3 accounts, the message will be moved to the Deleted Items folder, where it will remain until you empty your electronic trash. To empty the trash, click the Deleted Items folder, and then click Empty Deleted Items Folder.

Avoiding monotony. If remembering to purge the messages is a chore, you may want to configure Outlook Express to do it for you when you leave your IMAP folders. Just remember, once Outlook Express purges them, they're gone forever.

To set this option for your IMAP account, click Tools, and then select Options. In the Maintenance tab, place a check mark in the Purge Deleted Messages When Leaving IMAP Folders option. Click Apply and OK, and you're all set.

IMAP users will have messages marked for deletion, after which they'll have to click the Purge button (or select Edit, Purge Deleted Messages) to clean house. (See Figure 14.5 to learn what deleted messages will look like.)

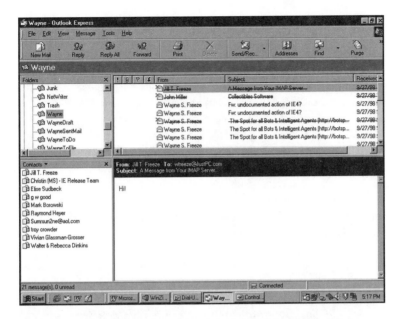

FIGURE 14.5 Messages marked for deletion will have a red "x" through their icons and a line drawn through their entries in the Message List.

Hey, it won't let me delete! This is one of those bizarre things that can make IMAP users crazy. Because the messages in your Inbox are stored on your mail server, you'll need to be connected to the server to process the deletions. If the connection dies unexpectedly, guess what? You'll keep hitting dead ends until you reconnect.

Then there are the messages that need further examination before you can delete them. Maybe the Subject line seems intriguing, but turns out not to interest you. Or maybe a Web site sends a weekly electronic newsletter that you read and then promptly delete.

Mastering multiple deletions You can save tremendous amounts of time and keystrokes by deleting multiple messages at once. To delete messages scattered throughout the Message List, click each message while holding down the Ctrl key, and then click Delete. To delete a group of contiguous messages, click the top one, press the Shift key, and then click the bottom one. All messages between the two points should be highlighted. Click Delete to delete them all.

In those cases, you'll most likely double-click the message to read it and then click the Delete button on the message toolbar when you're finished.

Uh-oh, I made a mistake! You may not be able to bring a message back once it's been deleted or purged from your system, but you can undo a deletion prior to exiting Outlook Express. Just right-click the message you marked by accident, and select Undelete from the shortcut menu. If the message has already been moved to the Deleted Items folder, you'll need to go there, right-click the mistakenly deleted message, and select Undelete from the shortcut menu. It's that easy.

Going, going, almost gone! Just because you delete an email message does not guarantee it's gone for good. Most corporations and government agencies perform routine backups of their networks. This means that a potentially damaging email message may come back later to haunt you.

Forwarding a Message

Say one of your co-workers sends you a great joke and you want to share it with a buddy. This is the perfect time to forward a message. The procedure is so easy. In fact, it doesn't even require a lengthy step-by-step walkthrough.

Double-click the message to open it if it isn't open already. Next, click the Forward Message button. A window similar to the New Message window will appear, only this window will include the entire text of the forwarded message as well.

All you need to do to send the message on its way is fill in the To: line using any of the methods described in Lesson 11, "Sending Email with Outlook Express," and then click the Send button. Before clicking Send, however, feel free to enter a personal message above the forwarded message.

 Protect your sources When you forward a message, the header information of the person who sent you the message is automatically included as well. If this is an important business associate or client, you may want to delete the header information to protect his privacy.

Replying to a Message

Replying to a message works similarly to forwarding a message. You click either Reply to Author or Reply All, add your message, and then click Send. Because you're responding to a message you received, there's no need to fill in the To: line—Outlook Express does it for you.

Saving a Message

No matter how much you try to avoid it, there will always be some messages you won't have the heart to part with, like that cute joke your nephew sent you. And in the case of the workplace, you'll find keeping a log of messages almost mandatory. If the messages remain in your Inbox until you delete them, your Inbox will become unmanageable sooner or later as a result of the sheer volume of messages. Furthermore, if you leave large numbers of messages on your IMAP mail server, you may "max out" your allocated disk space on your ISP's machine before you even realize it, which can lead to additional fees or problems. POP3 users avoid that worry altogether, because the messages are stored on the local machine once they've been downloaded.

With Outlook Express, you can save a message to your machine by simply leaving it in your Inbox, but it's probably a better idea to click its icon in the Inbox and drag it to a local folder to keep your Inbox down to a manageable size. In Lesson 18, "Locating a Specific Message in Outlook Express," I'll help you organize all those saved messages by creating folders in which to file them.

Checking for New Messages

By default, Outlook Express will automatically check for new email messages every half hour. You can ask it to refresh on demand by pressing the **F5** key or clicking the **Send and Receive** button, or you can adjust the time that elapses between automatic refreshes.

To adjust the time, follow these steps:

1. Click **Tools**, and then select **Options**.

2. Go to the **General** tab and look for the first item on the list, which should read Check for New Messages Every ___ Minute(s) (see Figure 14.6).

3. Use the arrow buttons to nudge the amount of time up or down as needed.

4. When you're satisfied with the number, click **Apply** to apply the change.

5. Click **OK** to save the change and close the dialog box.

In this lesson, you learned how to read and take action on all of your incoming email. Next, I'll help you get Outlook Express set up as a newsreader.

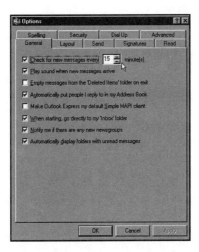

FIGURE 14.6 Use the arrow buttons to define the amount of time you want to pass between checks for new email.

Are you sure? It's very tempting to program frequent email checks. After all, none of us likes to miss anything, right? Well there's a distinct downside to frequent Inbox refreshes. First, it places an increased load on your Internet service provider's mail server, which may already be trying to service more people than it can be expected to handle. Second, the frequent checks can slow down other online activities. For instance, Web pages may load slower, RealAudio transmissions may experience static, and so on. Just give it careful thought before settling on a lower number.

LESSON 15

Setting Up Outlook Express to Be Your Newsreader

This lesson shows you how to turn Outlook Express into your personal newsreader.

Add a News Server to Outlook Express

Remember how you had to set up Outlook Express to recognize your mail server? The same holds true for news servers. Just follow these simple steps to make your newsreader available to Outlook Express:

1. Click the Outlook Express **Tools** menu and select **Accounts**. The Internet Accounts window appears.

2. Click the **Add** button and select **News** from the list. The Internet Connection Wizard launches.

3. The first screen asks you to enter your name as you want it to appear in the From field of your outgoing newsgroup posts. Type it in, and then click **Next**.

4. In the next screen, you are asked to provide your email address, which will be used in the Reply To line of any news articles you post. Click **Next**.

5. Next, you are asked to supply the name of your news server. You will also be asked whether or not you need to log on to the

newsserver. If you check the box, you'll be prompted to supply
your user ID and password.

6. See? This was even easier than setting up the email server—at
least there were fewer steps. Go ahead, click **Finish** to complete
the final step. You will then be asked whether or not you want to
download a listing of all the newsgroups available on the news
server you defined.

So How Do I Find the Good Stuff?

Because each person has a unique set of interests, it goes without saying
that our definitions of "the good stuff" will vary widely. Given that, I'll
have to show you how to find groups matching your interests instead of
pointing you to specific newsgroups.

There are numerous ways to find a good newsgroup, but here are a few of
the more reliable methods:

- **Word of mouth**—You seldom go wrong with newsgroups recommended to you by friends and associates. People like me,
  who've been cruising the Information Superhighway since it was
  a dirt footpath, tend to know which groups generate great dialog
  as opposed to spam-infested groups containing endless flame
  wars on off-topic subjects. (How's that for a nice image?)

> **Spam**   News articles or email that is irrelevant, unso-
> licited, and pushed out to a large number of news-
> groups or recipients. Some pieces of spam meet all
> three criteria.

- **Find it on the Web**   While researching a certain subject, you
  may wander across a Web site that's proven to be a wealth of
  information. Sites specializing in a topic will often point you to
  useful newsgroups. These are usually excellent leads to follow.

- **Search me**—Surf over to Deja News at `http://`
  `www.dejanews.com` and perform a search on a topic of interest.

The search results will reveal which groups discuss your topic of interest. Why is this potentially more useful than Outlook Express's newsgroup search function? Because newsgroup discussion topics aren't always covered in the name of the newsgroup. For example, if you ask Outlook Express to find newsgroups with Beanie Babies in their names, you won't get any hits (at least at the time this book was written). A newsgroup search on Deja News, however, reveals that Beanie Babies are discussed in `rec.toys.dolls`.

Flame war Generally, a flame war consists of a group of off-topic, potentially libelous messages that attack a poster's views or even something as simple as his or her spelling errors. (Makes you glad you got that Outlook Express spell checker, huh?)

- **Browse the list**—If you have eyes with great stamina, you may want to simply browse through the list of newsgroups available on your news server. To access this, launch Outlook Express and then click the name of your news server. A screen like the one shown in Figure 15.1 will appear, listing each newsgroup to which your Internet service provider subscribes. (If you've already subscribed to some newsgroups, you'll need to click the **Newsgroup** button on the right end of the toolbar to access this window.) Simply use the scrollbar to move through the list. And don't say I didn't warn you that it would be a lengthy proposition!

It's easy to get around! With the new Newsgroup Subscriptions window, not only is it easy to view the groups you subscribe to as well as newly created groups (click a tab at the bottom of the window), but also, managing multiple news servers is as simple as clicking the desired server's name.

My Internet Service Provider's
News Server

Microsoft's
Public News
Server

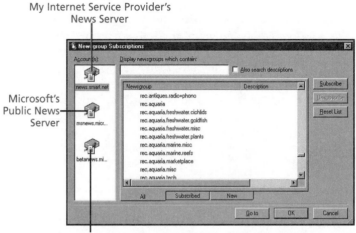

Microsoft's Secure Beta Tester Server

FIGURE 15.1   If you have multiple news servers set up, as seen here, you can manage any of them from this window by clicking their names.

- **Search the list**   Outlook Express lets you perform a search on the list of available newsgroups. To perform one, enter the desired term in the Display Newsgroups Which Contain: text box, and then click **Enter**. A list of newsgroups like the one shown in Figure 15.2 will be returned.

FIGURE 15.2   A newsgroup search should narrow the field of possibilities considerably.

It's not what it seems   Searching newsgroups isn't as straightforward as you might think. The reason? Think about how newsgroups are named—usually a string of words separated by periods, as in `misc.kids.vacation`. As such, you can't easily search a word in the traditional sense; you need to search for strings of characters. Take the search `cat`. A newsgroup search will return everything from *category* to *Catholic* to *cat* to even *education*. So how do you home in on what you want?

Checking the Also Search Descriptions box can help, but the search engine will still search a string of characters. That means you'll still have lots to sift through. One trick I've found that helps considerably is to include the period in the search, as in `.cat`. While you'll still find some irrelevant content, the number of items is reduced immensely.

Subscribing to a Newsgroup

Before you can subscribe to newsgroups, you'll need to make sure you have a list of those available on your computer. If the list doesn't appear when you access a news server, click the **Reset List** button.

While viewing the names of the newsgroups in the Newsgroup Subscriptions window, you can subscribe to a group using one of two methods. You can either double-click its name or click it to select it and click the **Subscribe** button. From that moment on, the groups you subscribed to will have a special icon next to their names (see Figure 15.3), and they will all appear in a separate window when you click the **Subscribed** tab at the bottom of the window. They will also appear on the File List in alphabetical order under the name of the news server.

If you're not certain you want to subscribe to the group, click it and then click the **Go To** button at the bottom-right part of the window. When you attempt to leave the newsgroup, Outlook Express will ask you if you want to subscribe or not.

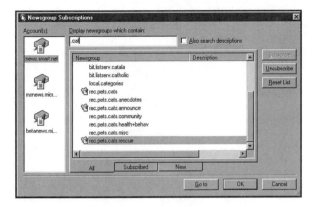

FIGURE 15.3   A special icon appears next to newsgroups to which you've subscribed.

Unsubscribing to a Newsgroup

When you no longer want to read the group on a regular basis, you may want to unsubscribe to it. To do this, simply right-click the newsgroup's name, and then click **Unsubscribe** on the shortcut menu. That's all there is to it.

With this lesson, you're all ready to begin exploring the tens of thousands of newsgroups that await you. Once you've gotten comfortable with how newsgroups work, you'll be ready to begin posting your own messages. I'll show you the ins and outs of doing this in the next lesson.

LESSON 16

Posting and Reading News Articles

This lesson shows you how to reply to articles you see, post your own articles, and retract posts you sent.

Reading a Newsgroup

You needn't subscribe to a newsgroup to read it. However, typically you will subscribe to a newsgroup when you go to read it.

 You never know what you may find out there All kinds of people frequent newsgroups these days. Given that, you should be prepared to encounter potentially offensive content while browsing. That's not to say you'll find racist or sexually explicit content everywhere you go, but you should know that it does exist so that you can protect your kids (and even yourself) from opening offensive messages.

Follow these steps to begin reading your favorite newsgroups:

1. Launch Outlook Express with a live connection to the Internet.

2. Scroll down your File List until you see the name of the newsgroup you want to read. If you cannot see the group on the list and a plus sign appears next to the name of the news server, you'll need to click the plus sign to expand the folders underneath the news server.

3. Double-click the newsgroup's name to begin reading. By default, messages are presented in the order they were posted, with the freshest being shown first. A plus sign next to the message means the message is part of a thread (an ongoing topic of discussion) and that there are responses to it that you can see by clicking the plus sign (see Figure 16.1 for an example of an expanded thread).

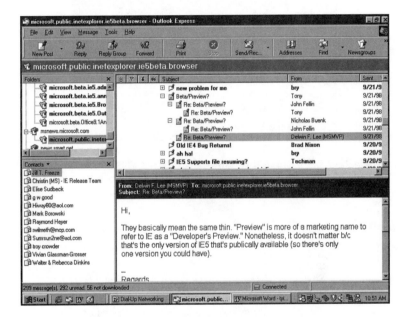

FIGURE 16.1   An example of just how involved a thread can become.

4. To begin reading a message, all you have to do is double-click it. The article appears in a window, similar to the one shown in Figure 16.2. Remember, if a plus sign appears next to a message, that means there are additional messages underneath it.

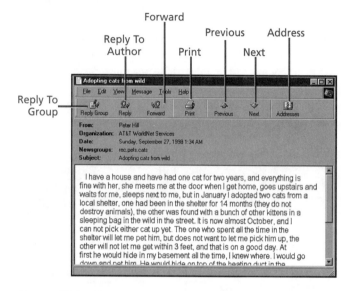

FIGURE 16.2   If you want to make the article's viewing area larger, you can do so by clicking on one of the window's border lines and pulling the window out in the desired location.

5. From within a message, there are multiple actions you can take on an article:

- **Save this Message**   Takes you to a traditional Save As dialog box. Note that you can save the message with a special newsgroup file extension (**.nws**) that must be viewed using Outlook Express, or you can choose a Text file (**.txt**) that can easily be viewed in Microsoft Word, WordPad, or the like.

- **Print**   Click this button to send the message to your default printer. Outlook Express will use its default settings, which should be fine in the majority of cases. If you want to have more control over your output, you'll want to click **File** and choose **Print** to access the Print dialog box. You have the same options available here as you did in Internet Explorer.

- **Reply to Group**   This button launches a Reply message window. Note that messages composed in this manner will be posted to the newsgroup for the entire world to see, as evidenced by the presence of the Newsgroup line item as opposed to the To: line. You compose the message just as you would a regular email message.

Netiquette notes   Before you respond to the group as a whole, make sure that what you have to say has value or interest to more people than just the original poster of the message to whom you're responding. Posting simple "me too" or "I agree" messages is generally frowned upon unless you are a noted expert on the subject. If the primary purpose of your note is to show the author your support, opt for Replying to Author instead.

Also, be sure to include enough of the message to which you're responding to give readers a context for your remarks. Otherwise, if it's not relevant, edit it out in the interest of saving bandwidth. Saving bandwidth basically decreases the amount of time needed to download a message and conserves the amount of space it takes up on mail servers.

- **Reply to Author**   Clicking this button routes your message directly to the author of the post to which you're responding. In fact, Outlook Express even inserts the author's email address and the subject line he or she used prefixed with an RE: for you. This is the best way to relate a relevant personal experience, show your support, or share an off-the-wall fact that may not be of general interest.

- **Forward**   If you want to send a newsgroup article to a friend or colleague via email, click this button, type in the person's email address (or double-click the To: icon to use an entry from your Address Book), add any notes you want to include, and then click Send.

- **Previous**   Click this button to view the message that came before the one currently being displayed.

- **Next**   To move to the next message in the list, click this button.

Posting Your Own Message to a Newsgroup

If, after much observation and research, you've decided to go ahead and post your question or comments to a newsgroup, follow these simple steps:

1. Click the folder of the newsgroup to which you'd like to post your message.

2. Click the New Message button on the Outlook Express toolbar. A standard New Message box opens, with the name of the selected newsgroup already filled in.

3. Want to crosspost to more than one newsgroup? If so, complete these steps to select additional newsgroups:

   - With the New Message window displayed, click Tools and choose Select Newsgroups, or click the Newsgroups icon in the Newsgroups line of the message. A dialog box like the one shown in Figure 16.3 appears.

   - Click a newsgroup you'd like to add to the list, and then click the Add button to place it in the list.

Open up a world of possibilities   By default, only the groups you are subscribed to appear in your list of choices. To view all possible groups, click the Show Only Subscribed Newsgroups toggle button. You may also want to use your newsgroup search techniques to locate desired groups here as well.

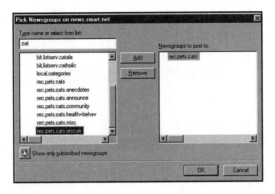

FIGURE 16.3   Use this box to select the newsgroups to which you'd like to crosspost.

- When your list is complete, click the **OK** button. All the groups you added to the list will be entered into the Newsgroups line.

Crossposting caution   Use extreme caution when posting the same message to multiple newsgroups. Posting off-topic messages to gobs of newsgroups at the same time is considered spamming (the mass posting or mailing of unsolicited or off-topic material), which can land you in a whole lot of hot water with your Internet service provider, not to mention a guarantee that you'll receive tons of angry email. It's best to crosspost when you're sure your message is acceptable to each newsgroup's charter, and when you think each group might have a slightly different "take" on your question or comment.

4. Type in the text of your message as you would with an email message. And don't forget to check your spelling.

5. When the message meets with your approval, click the **Post** button. Outlook Express will send you a message like the one pictured in Figure 16.4, saying your message is about to be sent to

the newsgroup server and that it may not show up immediately
in your display.

FIGURE 16.4   Click OK to confirm that you've read the message.

6. Click **OK** to close the message box and continue working in
Outlook Express.

Canceling an Article You Posted

Say you put a collectible up for sale in one of the newsgroups that allows
such posts, and you sell the item within a day. Canceling the post not only
reduces the load on news servers throughout the Internet, but it gives people one less article to browse, and it keeps you from having to send a million "I'm sorry, but I've already sold it" emails.

Before you begin, there's something else I should clarify. You can only
cancel articles you submitted, not articles from others that may be offensive or off the topic.

To recall or cancel an article you posted to a newsgroup, do the following:

1. Connect to the Internet and then open the newsgroup in which
you posted the article by clicking its name on your File List.

2. Find your article, and then right-click it. The shortcut menu
shown in Figure 16.5 appears.

3. Select **Cancel** from the menu. The message box shown in Figure
16.6 appears to let you know that the cancellation is in progress.

FIGURE 16.5   Choose Cancel to begin recalling your article from news servers around the world.

FIGURE 16.6   Click OK to let Outlook Express know you've read (and understand) this message.

 It takes time... Please note that this will not instantly remove your article from news servers around the world; this will take some time. You should also be aware that canceling a post will not remove it from the computers that may have already downloaded it with other messages from the same newsgroup. That means that someone who has read the newsgroup containing your post may have the article cached on his or her system, thus making it available even after you retract it.

4. Click OK to let Outlook Express know that you agree to the terms of the cancellation.

Viewing Replies to Your Post

If you're like most people, you want to see the replies to your posts as quickly as you can. In the past, you had to sift through the newsgroup with your bare eyes to find them. Now there's an easier way. By simply changing your view of a newsgroup's messages, you can see replies to your posts in a heartbeat. Here's how you do it:

1. Open the newsgroup in which you posted the message by clicking its name in the File List.

 Be sure the stuff is new   While you can do this offline as well, you may want to be sure that reasonably current data has been downloaded. If the download was processed significantly earlier, you'll want to perform it again to maximize your chances of seeing fresh responses to your post.

2. On the **View** menu, select **Current View, Replies to My Posts**.

3. A message window like the one you typically see will appear, but this window will display only your messages. Click the plus (+) sign to view all the headers of the posts nested under yours.

4. To return to the All Messages view, go to the **View** menu and select **Current View, All Messages** (or **Unread Messages**, if you prefer).

With a thorough knowledge of how to work with newsgroups, you're ready to tackle something a bit more advanced—viewing newsgroups offline using Outlook Express. In fact, that's the very next lesson in this book.

LESSON 17

Working with Outlook Express Offline

This lesson shows you how to process email and read newsgroups without being connected to the Internet.

Composing Email Messages Offline

Whether you want to free up your phone line or need to conserve time spent on the Internet, you may find it useful to compose messages offline. This means you can write as many messages as you want without tying up the phone line or burning up precious time on metered Internet service provider accounts. And while the term "offline" may sound a bit intimidating, it shouldn't be.

To begin composing messages offline, follow these simple steps:

1. Launch Outlook Express as you normally would, only you needn't connect to the Internet.

2. Begin composing an email message as you normally would, employing any or all of the techniques you learned in earlier lessons.

3. When you're finished, click **File**, and then select **Send Later**. The box in Figure 17.1 appears to tell you the message will be moved to the Outbox for mailing at a later time.

FIGURE **17.1**   This message box tells you the message you just composed will be placed in the Outbox for sending later.

4. Click **OK** to move the message to the Outbox.

5. To send the message(s), click the **Send and Receive** button on the Outlook Express toolbar.

6. You will be prompted to connect to the Internet and requested to provide your username and password information.

7. Outlook Express will make up to 10 attempts to connect to your mail server. Once it's established a connection, it will begin executing the tasks assigned, which will include sending the message(s) and checking for new email. You can either instruct Outlook Express to drop the connection when it's finished or you can maintain the connection to do some live Internet surfing.

But I'd like to do more with it...   If you aren't quite finished with the note, click **File, Save**. This action will save the note to your Drafts folder where you can easily retrieve it, edit it, and send it on when you have the time.

The World of Offline Newsreading

If you subscribe to more than a couple of newsgroups, the time spent online reading them can add up in a hurry. With Outlook Express, there's a way you can read newsgroups offline at your leisure, while freeing up the phone line for someone else.

There are essentially two ways to do this. The first method involves having Outlook Express download all of the messages for every newsgroup to which you subscribe. The download can take some time, but at least you have all of the articles at your fingertips.

The second method involves downloading only message headers, so you can get the gist of the current discussion and download only the messages you want. While doing it this way adds a few steps to the process, it can also save you time in that maybe you'll scrutinize what you want to read a bit more carefully if you have to purposely mark it for download. This second method is great for groups prone to massive amounts of spamming and those that routinely include only a small number of messages of interest to you. And you'll be happy to know you can combine the approaches as needed.

Preparing Newsgroups for Offline Browsing

Before you can begin reaping the rewards of offline browsing, you'll have to do a little setup work. Use the following steps as a guide in getting prepared:

1. Right-click the newsgroup that you'd like to set up first, and then select **Properties** from the shortcut menu.

2. Click the **Synchronize** tab of the Properties box to see the screen shown in Figure 17.2.

3. Place a check mark in the **When Synchronizing This Newsgroup, Download** box, and then choose the option that best fits your needs given the current group's content.

4. Click **Apply** to save the request, and then click **OK** to exit the dialog box.

5. Repeat these steps for each group you'd like to make available offline.

6. To download the specified information, click **Tools** on the menu bar, and then select **Synchronize**.

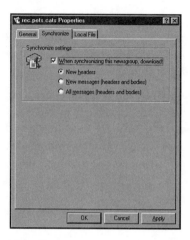

FIGURE 17.2   The Synchronize tab of the Properties dialog box is where you'll tell Outlook Express what to retrieve when you perform a newsgroup synchronization.

7. Disconnect from the Internet and begin browsing the newsgroups you've elected to download.

Downloading Certain Messages

If you opted to have Outlook Express download message headers only, you'll need to complete the following steps after performing the download of the headers:

1. In one of the newsgroups, click a message header that you'd like to read.

2. Click inside the mark for retrieval column (indicated by the downward pointing arrow icon shown in Figure 17.3).

Click here to mark a message for downloading.

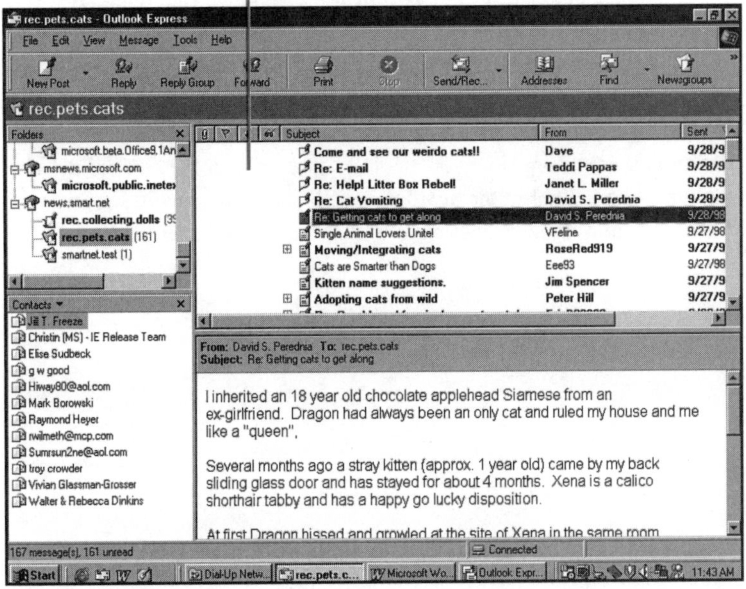

Figure 17.3 screenshot of Outlook Express showing the rec.pets.cats newsgroup with message headers and a preview pane displaying a message from David S. Perednia about getting cats to get along.

FIGURE 17.3   Click this column to mark a message for retrieval.

Know what you'll be getting   If you mark a message that has a plus sign next to it (is not expanded), you'll get the whole thread in a single mouse click. To get a single message only, expand the thread by clicking the plus sign, and then choose the post you want to read and follow the earlier steps for marking it.

3. Repeat these steps for each header whose message you want to read offline.

4. Next, click **Tools** on the menu bar, and then select **Synchronize**.

5. Disconnect from the Internet to minimize time spent online.

6. To assist in viewing the messages you chose to read, click **View** on the menu bar, select **Current View** and then **Downloaded Messages**. This will tell Outlook Express to display only the messages you marked for retrieval.

In this lesson, you learned how to take full advantage of offline email and newsgroup browsing. Now you needn't squabble over the availability of that lone phone line! In the next lesson, I'll show you how to sift through the enormous volume of messages to find the ones of interest.

LESSON 18

Locating a Specific Message in Outlook Express

This lesson shows you how to organize your messages and use Outlook Express' Find tool to locate the messages you want.

Getting Your Email Organized

Saving an email message may seem like a pretty basic task, and it is once you have Outlook Express all set up for it. But before you can tuck those valuable messages away, you'll need to create some folders in which to store them. Doing so will make it far easier for you find the messages you want without the use of complex search tools.

Follow these steps to create a folder for saved messages, move a message to its new location, and delete it from the Inbox:

1. Find a message you want to save and think about what type of folder you'd put it in if it were a physical piece of paper to be stored in a manila folder. It may be something like The Sudbeck Project, Humor, Recipes, Dissertation Notes, and so on.

2. Click **Local Folders** at the top of your Folders List pane to high-light it.

3. Click **File**, and then choose **Folder**, **New Folder**. The Create Folder dialog box shown in Figure 18.1 appears.

FIGURE 18.1   This is where you'll name each storage container for your messages.

4. Enter the name of the new folder, and then click **OK**. The new folder appears in alphabetical order in the Folder List pane.

5. Next, click the message you wish to move to the new folder and hold the mouse button down while dragging the message to its new location.

6. Once there, release the mouse button to drop the message into the folder. Outlook Express will automatically delete the message—or mark it as deleted in the case of IMAP servers—from your Inbox.

7. Repeat these steps as many times as needed until your filing system is all set up.

8. When you're finished moving everything, remember to clean up your Inbox by emptying the Deleted Items folder (POP3) or clicking **Edit** and selecting **Purge Deleted Messages** (IMAP).

After you've created all of the folders you need, saving messages will be a snap—just click and drag (or drag and drop as the current Microsoft buzz phrase goes) the message to its new location.

Filtering Email

One of the best ways to prevent a cluttered Inbox is to keep unwanted mail from coming in the first place. You can do this by making use of something called a filter.

Unfortunately, this feature, technically referred to as applying Message Rules, is only available for POP3 mail accounts, not those run off of IMAP servers. Microsoft has, however, at least agreed to look at making it available to IMAP users as well, so that's a start.

Message Rules are a powerful tool. In addition to sifting out some of the junk mail, they can perform a variety of functions, including the following:

- Automatically delete any messages coming from a specified source—a great way to kill repeat spam offenders before you're bothered by them even more.

 What's taking so long? If you merely filter spam into a Trash or Junk folder, you'll still be stuck with the download time. The only way to avoid this is to have Outlook Express delete the messages for you. Unfortunately, taking that action means you may miss a message that isn't really spam.

- If you maintain an FAQ for a certain topic or run a business where you'd like people to be able to request information, you can have Outlook Express automatically send a specified message back if the Subject line meets certain criteria. Best of all, you never have to see—much less handle—each request.

- Do you belong to a mailing list that generates oodles of messages? Why not have Outlook Express sort them for you so you can easily find important mail in your Inbox and quickly go to the special folder to find mailing list messages?

- Going out of town and need to have a co-worker deal with certain issues while you're out? Have messages automatically routed to your backup while you're away. That's right, Outlook

Express will actually forward messages with specified words in the Subject line, from a certain person, or whatever to the person you specify.

- Want to take a vote on a certain issue? Define a Yes folder and a No folder; tell people to use the appropriate word in the Subject line; define a message rule to route No responses to one folder and Yes responses to the other. You can effortlessly tally the results by clicking the folder and having Outlook Express add up the number for you. (When you open a folder, Outlook Express automatically tells you how many items are inside.)

Now that I've got you all fired up about using Message Rules, let's take a look at how to define them:

1. Click **Tools** in the Outlook Express menu bar and select **Message Rules, Mail**. The dialog box in Figure 18.2 appears the first time you attempt to create a message rule.

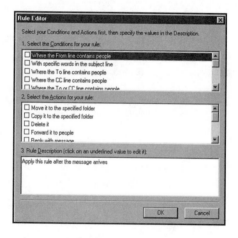

FIGURE **18.2**   The Rule Editor dialog box is where all the message rule selections are made.

2. The first thing the Rule Editor will ask you to define is the conditions for your rule. To do so, place a check mark next to any of the following conditions:

- Where the From line contains people

- With specific words in the subject line

- Where the To line contains people

- Where the CC line contains people

- Where the To or CC line contains people

- Where the message is from the specified account

- With specific words in the From line

- With specific words in the To line

- With specific words in the CC line

- With specific words in the To or CC line

- For all messages

3. Next, you'll be asked to tell Outlook Express which action you'd like it to take on messages that match the specified conditions. Just place a check mark next to any of these choices:

- Move it to the specified folder

- Copy it to the specified folder

- Delete it

- Forward it to people

- Reply with message

- Highlight with color

- Flag it

- Mark it as read

- Do not download it from the server

- Delete it from the server

4. In the Rule Description box, you'll be asked to elaborate on parts of the rule. For example, you may be asked to supply the word you wish to trigger the rule or the address to which qualifying messages should be routed. Just click the underlined word to see a box similar to the one shown in Figure 18.3.

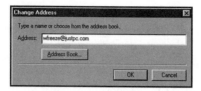

FIGURE 18.3   Among other things, you may be asked to provide an email address, depending on the conditions and actions you've specified.

5. After each underlined element has been supplied, click **OK**. The Message Rules dialog box reappears with a generic name for the rule (New Mail Rule #1) and a description of the actions to be taken under specified conditions.

6. To give the rule a more meaningful name, simply click it and begin typing the desired name.

Look what else you can do   Notice the buttons down the right side of the window. At any point, you can enter the Message Rules dialog box, click the desired rule, and either modify, rename, copy, or delete it.

7. Click **OK** when you're finished to complete the process.

The rules you just defined will be applied to messages as they reach your Inbox.

Finding a Newsgroup Message

Finding the messages that interest you the most in a newsgroup that generates hundreds of posts a day can be more than a little challenging. Outlook Express gives you a great way to sift through the oodles of material—the Find Messages tool.

To help you remember... If you tell Outlook Express to file certain messages for you, you may want to give the destination folders special codes to help yourself remember that Outlook Express is filing messages there. For example, if you join a specialized mailing list, you may define a rule that separates those messages from those sent specifically to you. In that case, you might want to name the folder rGoldens to specify that a rule (the "r" in the folder name) automatically puts messages from that mailing list there.

While I've geared these steps toward finding a newsgroup message, you should be aware that the same tool works for finding email messages stored on your machine. What a great way to uncover that ancient message where your boss promised you a promotion!

Follow these steps to locate a message in a newsgroup:

1. Click **Edit** and select **Find, Message**. The Find Message dialog box, pictured in Figure 18.4, appears.

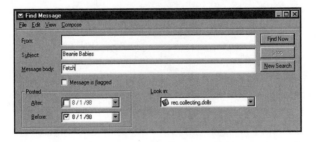

FIGURE 18.4   Fill in as many of the fields as you can to get the most applicable posts returned.

2. Unless you want to search every Outlook Express message (news and email), you'll want to click the **Browse** button to narrow the search.

3. Click the newsgroup you wish to search, and then click **OK**.

4. Fill in the field(s) you want Outlook Express to search: From, To, Subject, or Message. The more you fill in, the more applicable the results will be. Make sure your choices are accurate, though. If you have Outlook Express search for messages from the wrong sender, you won't get any results.

5. To narrow the time frame of your search and have fewer results returned, choose **Before** or **After** the date specified. If you want to use a date other than the one currently displayed, click the drop-down arrow to open a calendar from which you can choose an alternate date (see Figure 18.5).

FIGURE **18.5**   Double-click the date to insert it in the Date box.

6. Click the **Find Now** button. The results will be displayed at the bottom of the Find Message window, as shown in Figure 18.6.

7. Click the **Close** button (the **X** in the upper-right corner of the window) to resume working in Outlook Express.

In this lesson, I showed you all kinds of ways to find the messages you need. In addition, I presented some mail organizing tips and gave you a sneak peek at the powerful Message Rules tool.

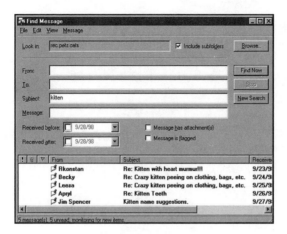

FIGURE 18.6   You can sort the results by clicking the column headers just as you can with email or general newsgroup browsing.

In the next lesson, we'll take a look at some Outlook Express housekeeping issues that will help you conserve valuable disk space and eliminate unwanted messages.

Outlook Express Housekeeping and Maintenance Issues

This lesson helps you make the most of Outlook Express' features to minimize wasted space on your computer.

Avoiding the Virtual Pack Rat Syndrome

By default, Outlook Express saves a copy of every message you send to the Sent Items folder. While this feature has saved my tail on more than one occasion by helping me remember what I've told whom, it can also quickly become a tremendous hog of disk space.

To rectify this potential problem, you may want to disable Outlook Express' Automatic Save feature and CC yourself in instances where you absolutely must keep a copy of the message.

Follow these steps to stop the automatic saves:

1. Click **Tools** on Outlook Express's menu bar and select **Options**.

2. Open the **Send** tab as shown in Figure 19.1.

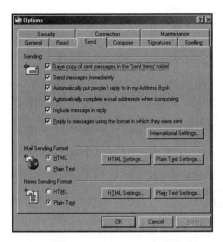

FIGURE 19.1   The Send tab is where you'll find all sorts of interesting mail options.

3. Remove the check mark next to the Save Copy of Sent Messages to the Sent Items folder.

Think before you send   Remember that after completing this transaction, you will no longer have copies of all the messages you send. If you want a copy, you'll have to list yourself on the CC line of a message.

---

4. Click Apply to save your changes, and then click OK to close the dialog box.

There's still some work to be done...   Changing this option does not remove the messages currently stored in your Sent Items folder. If you truly want to clean house, you'll need to go through the Sent Items folder, file the messages you want, and delete those you don't want.

Compact Mail Folders

Remember trash compactors? You'd throw gobs of garbage into them, press a button, and the garbage was magically smashed into a mass a fraction of its original size. Well, compacting mail folders uses a similar concept. You tell Outlook Express to suck it in and cram everything as close together as it can. This may not help you regain gigabytes of space, but there are times when every little bit helps.

To begin compacting mail folders, select the folder you want to compact first and click **File, Folder, Compact**. In a few seconds, the job will be done. You can also opt to use the Compact All Folders command to save yourself some time and mouse clicks.

Marking Newsgroup Messages as Read and Viewing Only New Posts

One of the more basic ways to trim down the Message List for a newsgroup involves marking messages as Read and then changing the current view to reflect only new messages. This will make skimming the messages much more efficient and will undoubtedly free up disk space on your machine. Once you've gone through these steps for each newsgroup, you'll be set for the long run, because you'll always have fewer messages with which to deal.

To mark messages as Read and change the current view, follow these steps:

1. Connect to the Internet and launch Outlook Express as you would if you were going to read the newsgroups online.

2. Click the name of the first group you'd like to browse.

3. Begin reading the messages of interest. Note that Outlook Express automatically marks messages previewed for 5 seconds or longer as Read.

Tweaking the number   If you feel the 5-second setting doesn't quite work for you, you can adjust it by
opening the **Tools** menu and then selecting **Options**
and choosing the **Read** tab as shown here. In the
Message Is Read After Previewing for ___ Seconds line,
use the arrow buttons to nudge the amount of time
up or down as desired.

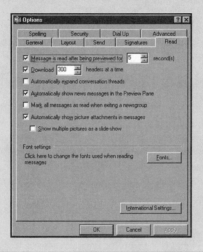

4. When you've finished going through the entire group, open the
Edit menu and select **Mark All as Read**.

K.I.S.S.   Keep it simple—save. If there are messages
you think you'll want to see again, save them. That
way you won't have to return to All Messages view
and wind your way through thousands of messages.

5. Next, you'll want to change your current view so that Outlook
Express will display only unread messages. Click **View** and then
select **Current View, Unread Messages**. A lot fewer messages

appear, huh? In fact, the display may remain empty until you refresh it by pressing **F5**.

6. When you leave Outlook Express and return at a later time, you'll only see new messages in the Message List display.

 Restoring the view If you want to see all current messages again, whether they've been read or not, open the **View** menu and then select **Current View, All Messages**.

Remove Old News Messages

Outlook Express currently stores news messages up to five days old on your machine for quick retrieval. If you feel newsgroup articles are taking up far too much space on your system, you might want to reduce the number of days worth of messages that are stored locally.

To do this, open the **Tools** menu, select **Options**, and then click the **Advanced** tab (see Figure 19.2).

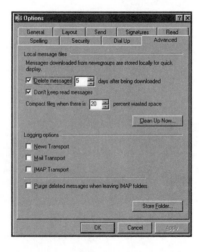

Figure 19.2 The Advanced tab is where you'll specify the allowed age of news articles stored locally.

In the Delete Messages ___ Days After Being Downloaded line, use the arrow buttons to reduce the number of days allowed.

Compact Stored Messages

Remember my trash compactor analogy from earlier in this lesson? Well, you can do the same with stored newsgroup messages. Just follow these simple steps:

1. Find the newsgroup in the file list you'd like to compact first.

2. Right-click its name and select **Properties** from the resulting shortcut menu.

3. Choose the **Local Files** tab as shown in Figure 19.3. Look at the amount of wasted disk space.

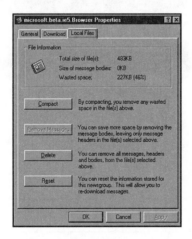

FIGURE 19.3   The newsgroup shown here has 46% wasted disk space; time to compact the files!

4. Click the **Compact** button. Outlook Express will go to work to reduce that percentage of wasted disk space to zero.

5. Repeat these steps to clean up each newsgroup for which you have messages stored on your machine.

You always have options   The Local Files tab also gives you the opportunity to remove message bodies to save space (the Remove Messages button) or to delete complete messages (the Delete button).

This lesson presented a number of ways to help you regain wasted disk space on your computer. In the next lesson, we shift our attention to something radically different—developing Web pages using FrontPage Express.

LESSON 20

Building Web Pages with FrontPage Express

This lesson introduces you to Web page design basics using a special member of the Internet Explorer 5 suite—FrontPage Express.

Learning the Lay of the FrontPage Express Land

As I've done throughout the book, I'd like to present the application's workspace using a screen shot with callouts (see Figure 20.1). This will help you quickly learn just which buttons are located where. You'll almost instantly notice that you've encountered a bunch of the buttons before in Outlook Express (or in Word if you use Microsoft Office).

The title bar and the menu bar serve the same functions here as they do in other applications covered throughout this book. Even the Formatting toolbar is nearly identical.

Menu bar

Title   Forms   Standard   Format
bar   toolbar   toolbar   toolbar

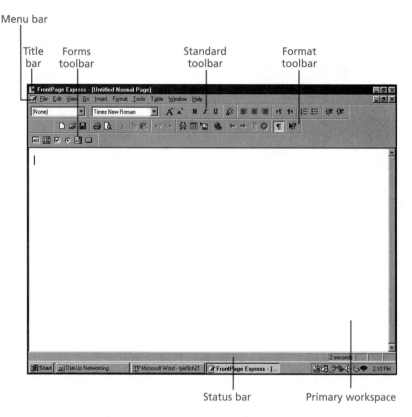

Status bar   Primary workspace

Figure 20.1   The FrontPage Express workspace.

Formatting Web Page Text

One main feature of a Web page is its computer platform independence. A
Web page built on a Windows 98 machine can be viewed by Windows 95,
Windows 3.1, Macintosh, UNIX, and any other system with a basic
browser. To reach this degree of universal accessibility, text in Web pages
uses formatting styles rather than specific font sizes—point size—as in a
word processing program. In FrontPage Express, headings used for titles
and subtitles can range in size from the largest (Heading 1) to the smallest
(Heading 6).

Follow these steps to enter and format some text on your Web page:

1. Start FrontPage Express. Depending on how your machine is configured, you may have to dig for it a little. Most commonly, the application can be found by clicking **Start** and then choosing **Programs, Accessories, Internet Tools**.

2. Type in your first heading.

3. Select the text you just entered by clicking in front of it and dragging the mouse across the rest while holding down the left mouse button.

4. From the **Change Styles** box in the toolbar, click the arrow to reveal the drop-down options list (see Figure 20.2).

Click here to view your Style options.

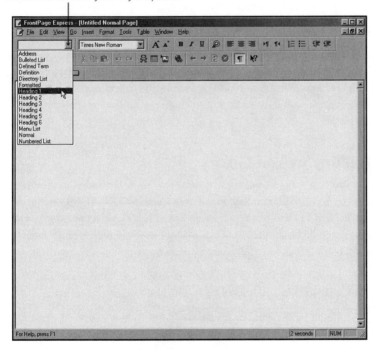

FIGURE 20.2   The Change Styles box helps you select your text style and size.

5. From the **Options** list, click a text style choice. Heading 1 or Heading 2 is suitable for a Web page title. The text changes to reflect the selected size.

6. Keeping the text highlighted, click one of the Alignment buttons to make the text align to the left, centered, or right. By default, the text will be aligned left.

7. If desired, click the standard **Bold**, **Italic**, or **Underline** style button.

8. Click anywhere on the blank page to clear the highlight and continue working in FrontPage Express.

Repeat these steps to continue adding text to your Web page, varying the text styles between Headings and Normal.

Linking: What the Web's All About

Whether it's links between multiple pages you created or links to your favorite Web sites, links are a fundamental part of Web site development. In the sections that follow, you'll learn how to connect pages within your Web site, and you'll discover how to connect your site to others around the world.

Linking as You Go

The simplest way to create links within your own Web site is to create them as you build them. Say one of your interests is NASCAR racing. Maybe you'd like to build your own page of NASCAR-related links. It's simplest to highlight the NASCAR racing bullet and then create the new page. Skim through the following steps to see why this way is easiest:

1. Launch FrontPage Express and open the page from which you wish to create additional pages or links.

2. Highlight the word or phrase you'd like to turn into a link. This is where the reader will click to be taken to the new page.

3. From the FrontPage Express **Insert** menu, select **Hyperlink**.

4. Click the **New Page** tab of the Create Hyperlink dialog box to
   see the screen shown in Figure 20.3.

FIGURE 20.3   FrontPage Express will attempt to create a new page
title and URL for the page you're about to create.

5. FrontPage Express will automatically enter a title for the new
   page and create a URL based on the text you highlighted. If you
   don't like the name FrontPage Express has created, feel free to
   change it by clicking inside the appropriate text box and typing
   in new information.

6. When you're satisfied with the page title and URL name, click
   the **OK** button.

7. In the New Page dialog box shown in Figure 20.4, select
   Normal Page.

FIGURE 20.4   Notice that you can create all kinds of Web pages
using FrontPage Express.

8. Click the **OK** button, and FrontPage Express will display a brand new blank page that you can begin designing to your heart's content.

Linking to Other Web Sites

There are oodles of valuable resources on the Internet (and oodles more that are just plain fun to visit). In light of that fact, you'll want to be sure you know how to create links from your Web page to other Web pages.

Before I jump into the steps, there are a couple of things you can do to make the process run more smoothly. As you execute the steps to link to another Web site, you'll discover you need to enter the URL of the Web site to which you'd like to link.

It's a little more complicated than that. If the Web site's address is short and you can remember it off the top of your head, typing it in is no problem. If, on the other hand, it's a long, cumbersome one or you can't remember it, you'll need to establish a connection to the Internet, fire up Internet Explorer, open the Web site, and copy and paste its URL into the dialog box as described next.

 Copy and paste? In case you need a quick refresher course on some Windows program editing basics, here it is. When you have the Web page you want to link to displayed in Internet Explorer, click inside the Address Box. The whole URL should be highlighted. (If for some reason it's not, you can always click at the far left end and drag the mouse to the opposite end to select the entire address.) After the URL is highlighted, right-click it and select Copy from the shortcut menu. You'll paste it in as directed later by right-clicking the text box described next (see step 6) and choosing Paste from the shortcut menu.

Follow these steps to connect your Web page to another Web site:

1. If needed, connect to the Internet to pull up the necessary URL.

2. Launch FrontPage Express, load the page you want to edit, and highlight the text you want to turn into a hyperlink.

3. From the **Insert** menu, choose **Hyperlink**.

4. Select the **World Wide Web** tab in the Create Hyperlink dialog box. (This is the tab that should open by default.)

5. Use the drop-down arrow if needed to make sure the Hyperlink Type is defined as http: (see Figure 20.5). You'll notice that the appropriate http:// prefix appears in the URL box.

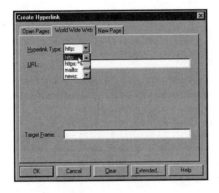

FIGURE 20.5   Use the drop-down arrow and scrollbars to make sure the desired link type is selected.

6. Next, enter the desired URL into the URL box by either typing it or copying and pasting it as described in the previous Note.

7. Click **OK** when you're finished to complete the link.

Believe it or not, you can also use these same steps to link to email addresses (as in "Please email Jill Freeze [where Jill Freeze is a link to my email address] for additional information.").

To do this, follow the previous steps, but this time select **mailto:** as the link type. Then all you have to do is enter the appropriate email address in

the URL box. Linking to a special newsgroup is just as easy—choose
news: as the link type, and then enter the group's name in the URL box.

Including Images on Your Web Page

The steps you'll need to follow to include an image on your Web page are
fairly straightforward. Just do the following:

1. Open the Web page to which you want to add an image.

2. Click in the location you want to place the image.

3. From the **Insert** menu, select **Images** to open the Image dialog
   box, shown in Figure 20.6.

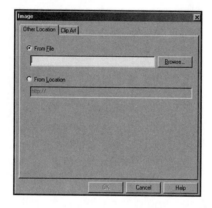

FIGURE 20.6   The Browse button lets you access any image on your
computer.

4. With the **Other Location** tab open, click the **Browse** button to
   click your way to the file you want to add.

5. When you find the file you want, double-click its name to return
   to the **Other Location** tab. Click **OK** to exit the dialog and put
   the image in its place.

The need for speed If you plan to use an image repeatedly throughout your Web site (as might be the case with a graphical logo), consider clicking the From Location option on the Other Location tab and entering the URL of the image. That way, you can store the image in one location as opposed to each page (which saves you space on the Web server for other goodies), and it dramatically reduces the image download time for your visitors.

Publishing Your Web Page

Most Internet service providers prefer that you save your Web page to their FTP server. To do this, take the following steps:

1. Open the page you want to place on the Web in FrontPage Express.

2. Open the File menu and select Save As. The Save As dialog box appears, displaying the name and location of your Web page file.

3. Click OK. If you used any images or other files in your Web page, a dialog box appears asking if you want to save these files to the Web server (see Figure 20.7).

FIGURE 20.7   FrontPage Express will prompt you to add any extra files you used to the current Web folder.

4. Click Yes to All. The Web Publishing Wizard launches and then overlays an Enter Network Password dialog box.

5. Type your username in the Username text box, tab to the Password text box, and type your password. Click OK.

The memory of an elephant... FrontPage Express is set up to save your password, so you won't need to enter it the next time you publish a Web page. Hey, anything to make life a little easier, right?

6. The Web Publishing Wizard reappears, displaying an explanation of what you are about to do. Click Next.

7. You are first asked to select your connection method. By default, **FTP** should be selected. Click Next.

8. Type the name of your FTP server (and the name of the subfolder containing your Web pages if applicable). Click Next.

9. The wizard tells you it's ready to publish your page. Click **Finish** to proceed.

When a problem occurs... If you should encounter a problem while trying to publish your Web page, you may need to verify that you entered the necessary information correctly on the Web Publishing Wizard. If you still run into problems, consult your ISP for assistance.

This lesson only scratches the surface of what you can do with FrontPage Express. You can also change the color of your text and background, add sound files, include graphics, and so on. You can learn more about some of these features by browsing *Sams Teach Yourself Microsoft Internet Explorer 5 in 24 Hours*. Next, I'll introduce you to NetMeeting, another fun and useful tool included with the Internet Explorer 5 suite of applications.

Lesson 21

Communicating with Others in Real-Time Using NetMeeting

This lesson gives you a brief introduction to the many uses of NetMeeting.

Getting to Know Microsoft NetMeeting

At first glance, it may seem like NetMeeting is for corporate executives, with minimal application for the casual user. Not true. My kids Christopher and Samantha love doing group art projects using the NetMeeting whiteboard (see Figure 21.1). But there's much more to NetMeeting than that.

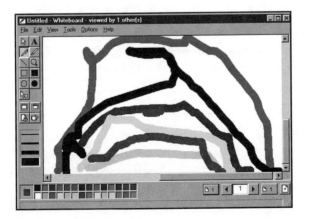

Figure 21.1   Five-year-old Christopher draws Mommy a rainbow while helping her test the new NetMeeting.

Does the thought of free long distance telephone calls appeal to you? (Well, maybe not if you're a telephone company executive, but....) Do you occasionally telecommute from home so you can spend more time with your family? Or maybe you want to compare your Barbie doll collection inventory with a friend's across the country. And finally, what if you're part of a work group stationed at different sites? You could really use a good real-time collaborating tool.

 Always be prepared   To experience the full value of NetMeeting, you should have a microphone, sound card, and speakers properly installed on your system.

Sure, you could set up a chat room somewhere, but what do you do if you want to brainstorm or collaborate on an important document? NetMeeting is the answer. Not only can you use NetMeeting as a simple chat application, you can turn it into an Internet phone, work on a document with an associate across the globe, or sketch out the company's reorganization on the NetMeeting whiteboard.

In the sections that follow, I'll help you get NetMeeting set up and show you how to begin working with each of NetMeeting's major components.

Setting Up NetMeeting

When you launch NetMeeting for the first time, the NetMeeting Setup Wizard will greet you. Like many of the other Microsoft wizards, the NetMeeting Setup Wizard exists to make an otherwise intimidating task easier.

 Close up shop before you begin!   Before you begin configuring NetMeeting, close any other programs you may have open. You'll be tweaking some of your computer's audio settings and won't want any interference from other programs you may be running.

Follow these steps to get NetMeeting ready for business (or pleasure):

1. Launch NetMeeting by clicking the **Start** button on the Windows taskbar and then clicking **Programs, Internet Explorer, Microsoft NetMeeting.**

2. Read the introductory screen, and then click the **Next** button to begin configuring the program. The dialog box in Figure 21.2 appears.

FIGURE 21.2   Choose the directory server you'd like NetMeeting to automatically log onto upon launching.

3. This dialog box asks if you want to log onto a directory server automatically and, if so, which one. Since it could come in handy when trying to find someone else online, I suggest letting it log onto the default server for now. You can always change it later should the need (or desire) arise. Click **Next** to continue.

4. NetMeeting will ask you to provide information about yourself that can be accessed by other users. While you'll need to provide at least your first name, last name, and email address to proceed with the setup, you should use caution when providing the optional information. Remember, you have no control over who may access this information, so the less that's offered, the better. Enter the information you'd like to make available in the corresponding text boxes, and then click **Next** to move on.

> **But the Wizard doesn't pop up every time I launch NetMeeting; how do I change the server I use?** Click the Tools menu item on the NetMeeting toolbar, and then click Options. Open the Calling tab. You can change the server you access by default in the top section of this screen, using the drop-down arrow. You can also select a new directory server on-the-fly by using the Server drop-down arrow on the main NetMeeting screen. Changing it here, however, doesn't change the server that opens upon NetMeeting's launch.

5. You will then be asked to classify your use of NetMeeting. Is it for business use? Family use? Adults-only communication? Only you can decide which option is the most appropriate. Select one, and then click Next.

6. The next order of business is to tell NetMeeting about your connection to the Internet. Choose the appropriate option, and then click Next.

7. NetMeeting tells you that you are about to configure the audio portion of NetMeeting. Close any other programs you have running that play sounds, and then click Next to continue.

8. The Audio Tuning Wizard opens to help you verify that your sound card is configured properly for use with NetMeeting. Click the Test button to hear the sample sound, and click and drag the Volume lever up or down as necessary. When you're satisfied, click the Stop button and then click Next.

9. Next, you'll set up your microphone for use with NetMeeting. Click the Start Recording button and begin reading aloud the paragraph provided. Remember to speak clearly and loudly into the microphone as you would when placing a NetMeeting phone call.

Pump up the volume! While it's true that many laptops come with built-in microphones, they may not be quite up to the task of frequent NetMeeting use. If you plan to use the application to make Internet phone calls often, you may want to consider upgrading to a higher quality microphone that attaches to your computer.

10. When the Audio Tuning progress status bar reaches the end, NetMeeting will stop recording. Click Next. You don't need to finish reading the entire paragraph; it's just there for you to give NetMeeting a speech sample. This is what it uses to adjust the sensitivity of the microphone.

11. A screen will appear, telling you that the setup is complete. Click Finish to have NetMeeting dial up the directory server you specified.

The NetMeeting Workspace

By now you should know how I feel about setting the stage before jumping into using an application. That is, you shouldn't be at all surprised by the fact that I want to acquaint you with NetMeeting's workspace.

Figure 21.3 illustrates NetMeeting's basic work area as it will appear while connected to a directory server.

Microsoft NetMeeting has some traditional Windows application elements—a title bar, a menu bar, a toolbar, and a status bar. It also has some unique elements like audio level controls, a directory listing, some navigation buttons, and the Category and Server lists. Because the typical elements need no explanation (you've heard me talk about them endlessly already, right?), we'll shift our focus to NetMeeting-specific elements.

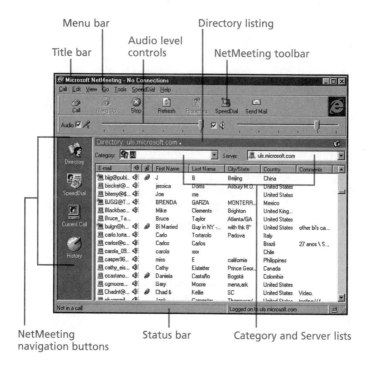

FIGURE 21.3   The Microsoft NetMeeting workspace.

The audio level controls are probably the first new element that will grab your attention. These controls include two sliders that you can use to tweak the volume of your voice or the voice of a caller. Just click and drag the microphone slider to the right to increase the volume of your voice. Do the same for the speaker slider to increase the volume of a caller's voice.

Next, you'll see the Category and Server lists. Use the Category drop-down arrow to change the category of people viewed onscreen. The Server list lets you switch to another directory server to see who may be logged on there.

The largest new element is the Directory listing, which takes up a good portion of the NetMeeting screen. This area displays information about others logged on to the selected directory server in the chosen category (the personal, business, or adults-only distinction). The fields displayed are listed in Table 21.1.

TABLE 21.1   Fields Available for Viewing in the Directory Listing

Field Name	Contents
E-mail	The person's email address.
Audio	A small yellow speaker appears if the person has audio capabilities.
Video	A small gray video camera will be displayed for users with video capabilities.
First Name	The person's first name as he or she entered it on the Personal Information tab.
Last Name	The person's last name—some opt to type in a fictional last name to protect their privacy.
City/State	Where the person is located.
Country	Name of the country from which the listed person is calling.
Comments	Notes about the interests of the person or the topic he or she wants to discuss with others.

Putting things in order   By default, NetMeeting will display the names of those logged on to the directory server in alphabetical order by email address. You can sort by any other field as well by clicking its header. As always, you can reverse the order of the sort by clicking the column header a second time.

Finally, we have the NetMeeting navigation buttons, which we'll look at in greater detail later in the lesson.

Making a Call Using NetMeeting

Think about the steps you have to go through when placing a call the traditional way. You have to first remember the phone number of the person you want to call or, heaven forbid, look up their number in the telephone book. Then you have to dial the number.

The task is much simpler with NetMeeting. If you have a sound card, a set of speakers, and a microphone inside of or attached to your computer, you can engage in voice conversation with as little as a double-click of the mouse.

Follow these steps to place your first NetMeeting call:

1. Launch NetMeeting as described earlier in this lesson.

2. If the person you want to call is listed with the directory server you've defined to launch upon the application's start, just use the scrollbars to find his or her entry in the Directory list. If it's not the same server, use the Server drop-down box to change the server you're logged on to.

3. When the person's name is in view, double-click it to place the call. The person will have the option to accept or ignore your call.

4. If he or she accepts your call, you will be connected within seconds.

5. If he or she doesn't accept your call, you will have the option of leaving a message. Click **Yes** to launch Outlook Express with a New Message window pre-addressed to the person you attempted to call.

6. While you're connected, you can engage in a variety of NetMeeting functions, including audio chat, text chat, document sharing, and whiteboard drawing.

7. Click **Hangup** to end the call.

The Current Call window (Figure 21.4) has a number of columns that provide information about those to whom you are connected.

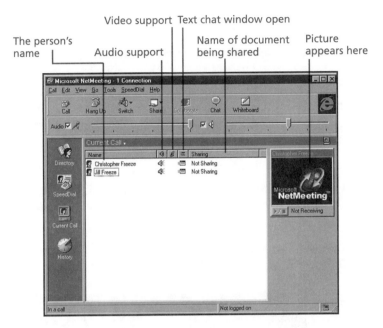

FIGURE 21.4   The Current Call pane will provide a host of valuable information.

Receiving a Call

If you thought making a NetMeeting call was easy, just wait until you see how simple it is to answer one! And you don't even have to go on a scavenger hunt for the misplaced cordless phone.

When you receive a call, a small dialog box will appear near the Windows taskbar. It'll say something like "You have an incoming call from Samantha Freeze. Would you like to accept it?" The dialog box has two buttons you can click—one for accepting the call and one for ignoring it. Clicking **Accept** immediately moves you to the Current Call view, as shown back in Figure 21.4.

Participating in a NetMeeting Text Chat

If you see that the person who has called you doesn't have audio support (or you yourself do not have audio capabilities), a text chat may be in order. It's also a great way to correspond silently in real-time so others don't hear you. It's not as entertaining as Microsoft Chat, but it definitely serves the purpose.

To begin a text chat, follow these steps:

1. Once you've called someone (or they've called you), verify that you're in Current Call view. (You can always click the **Current Call** navigation button to make sure that you are.)

2. Click the **Chat** button on the **Current Call** toolbar. The screen in Figure 21.5 appears.

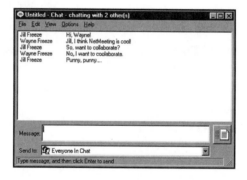

FIGURE 21.5   The NetMeeting Chat screen.

3. Type your message in the Message text box, and then press **Enter**. The entire conversation will appear in the large pane immediately above the Message box.

4. When you've finished chatting, simply close the Chat window by clicking the **X** in the upper-right corner of the window. NetMeeting will alert others that you have left the chat area.

Using the Whiteboard to Communicate Ideas

When my husband managed a large computer center for a major university, he was famous for all the scribblings on his wall-size whiteboard. In meetings, it allowed the staff to brainstorm in a way that everyone could see the output. You can do the same thing from afar with the NetMeeting whiteboard.

If you think it's complicated, think again! Admittedly, I never played with NetMeeting until I started writing *Sams Teach Yourself Microsoft Internet Explorer 5 in 24 Hours*. We loaded it onto all four computers on our home's local area network (LAN). My five-year-old son immediately took a shine to the whiteboard and the ability to draw and paint in a variety of colors. When I first started playing with the program, I couldn't figure out how to make the shapes. My son came up to me, watched me a couple of minutes, and said, "No, Mommy, you click the shape, click here (points to the whiteboard), and then drag the mouse out." That's right. NetMeeting's so easy to use, even a five-year-old can do it.

While we don't have time in this lesson to explore every little detail about the whiteboard, you can learn a lot in a very little time.

Figure 21.6 presents the NetMeeting whiteboard with callouts pointing to key buttons.

Take some time to play around with the whiteboard a bit. I think you'll find it a lot easier to work with than you may have imagined.

In this lesson, you got a quick overview of what NetMeeting can do. Our final lesson explores the unique Microsoft Chat environment.

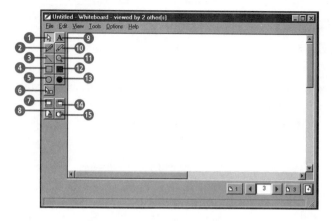

FIGURE 21.6   The whiteboard's workspace.

❶ Selector
❷ Text
❸ Pen
❹ Highlighter
❺ Line
❻ Zoom
❼ Unfilled rectangle
❽ Filled rectangle

❾ Unfilled ellipse
❿ Filled ellipse
⓫ Eraser
⓬ Select window
⓭ Select area
⓮ Lock contents
⓯ Remote pointer on

LESSON 22

Chatting on the Internet Using Microsoft Chat

This lesson shows you how to chat with others as an unusual comic strip character.

What's the Deal With Microsoft Chat?

Microsoft Chat is no ordinary chat program. Sure, you can use it to participate in regular IRC text chats too, but its primary difference lies in its ability to let people chat as cartoon characters. That's right, you and a few of your closest friends can star in your own comic strip—a comic strip just like the ones found in the Sunday paper, complete with conversation balloons and all (see Figure 22.1).

FIGURE 22.1 Microsoft Chat's comic strip format adds life to online chatting.

If you are chatting with someone else who happens to use Microsoft Chat as his or her chat software, you'll both see the characters each of you designed. If the other chat participants do not use Microsoft Chat, characters will be automatically defined for each of them so you'll still witness the chat in comic strip view.

Getting Ready to Chat with Microsoft Chat

In exchange for the added personality brought to your chat, you'll have a bit more setup work to do before you begin. You'll need to provide information about yourself, choose your comic strip character, choose the character's background scene, and then connect to a chat server.

Providing Information About Yourself

Of course, before you begin setting up Microsoft Chat, you'll need to launch the program. To do this, click the Start button on the Windows taskbar, and then choose Programs, Accessories, Internet Tools, Microsoft Chat. A Chat Connection dialog box with two tabs appears.

Chat Server To participate in a chat using Microsoft Chat, you'll need to connect to something called a chat server. This is a machine that passes messages between participants in a chat. After all, we need someone—or something—to keep track of who should receive our messages and who should not, right?

While the Connect tab is the tab you'll see first, there are some things you'll want to do before establishing a connection to the chat server. One of these things consists of entering information about your real identity and personal interests. Follow these steps to provide this information for fellow chatters:

1. Click the **Personal Info** tab on the Chat Connection dialog box. The screen shown in Figure 22.2 appears.

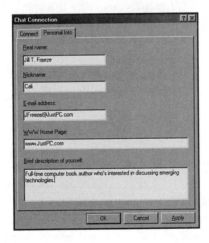

FIGURE 22.2 Other chatters can request the information you provide on this tab.

2. In the first field, provide your real name if you choose.

3. The Nickname field lets you choose the name you'll be known by onscreen. When you log on to the chat server, you'll be told if your chosen nickname is already in use.

4. Next, you are asked to type in your email address in the field provided.

They'll know where to find you   Remember that other chatters can access this information to contact you outside of the chat room.

5. If you have a personal Web page you'd like others to visit, just enter its address in the WWW Home Page text box.

6. Finally, you are asked to provide a brief description of yourself.

Better to say something than nothing!   Whatever you do, don't leave the description field blank. If you do, the words "This person is too lazy to create a profile entry" will appear, thanks to Microsoft. At bare minimum, I suggest you erase this line, even if you don't want to share any additional information.

7. When you've finished entering all the data you want to include, click the Apply button to save the information.

Establishing a Chat Identity

Picking your special character and background can be a whole lot of fun. Just follow these steps:

1. With Microsoft Chat up and running, click View, Options from the menu bar. A multi-tabbed Microsoft Chat Options dialog box opens. You'll recognize the Personal Info tab from the setup steps you followed. Click the Character tab to reveal the screen shown in Figure 22.3.

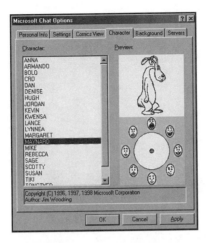

FIGURE 22.3 Click a name to view its corresponding character.

2. Click a character's name to see its picture in the Preview pane. You can choose from a variety of characters, from a curvaceous dark-haired woman to a scruffy bathrobe-clad cat.

If you're happy and you know it... Want to see what the character you selected looks like displaying a variety of emotions? Click the faces in the emotion wheel below the Preview pane to take a look.

3. Click **Apply** to save your choice of character.

4. Next, select the **Background** tab on the Microsoft Chat Options dialog box to see the screen shown in Figure 22.4.

5. Click the background names to preview them until you find the one you want to use.

6. Press **Apply** to save your selection.

7. Now it's time to connect to a chat server. Click the **Connect** tab to get started.

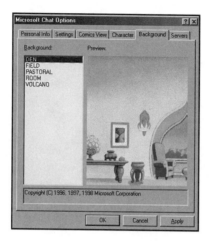

FIGURE 22.4 Click the name of the background you want, and then see what it looks like in the Preview pane.

8. There are multiple ways to specify a chat server. They include the following:

   • Use the drop-down arrow next to the Favorites text box to locate a room previously saved as a Favorite.

> **Find something you like?** While participating in a favorite chat room, click the Favorites menu and choose Add to Favorites. The chosen room will be instantly accessible next time you want to chat.

   • Use the drop-down arrow by the Server box to choose one of Microsoft's servers.

   • Click inside the Server box and type in the name of the chat server you want to access.

9. Once you've chosen the server, you need to select a chat room in which to participate. Press the **Go to Chat Room** button if you know the name of the chat room you want to go to, or the **Show All Available** button to choose from the list of rooms currently available on the chosen server.

10. Click **OK** to make the connection. You're ready to begin chatting!

 Someone's shooting blanks! Don't be shocked if your viewing panel is blank when you first enter the chat room. Microsoft Chat picks up only conversation that occurs when you enter the room, not that which occurred before.

Understanding the Microsoft Chat Environment

At first glance, Microsoft Chat may appear intimidating because of its multiple panels and dozens of buttons. But once you know your way around, you'll find them a convenience rather than a clutter.

Let's start by exploring the main chat area. In Figure 22.5, you'll notice that there are several key elements in the Microsoft Chat workspace. I've identified them with callouts to make it absolutely clear which element is which, and I've defined their purposes in Table 22.1.

TABLE 22.1 Microsoft Chat Workspace Elements and Their Purposes

Element	Purpose
Viewing pane	This, the largest area of the Microsoft Chat workspace, is where you'll see the comic strip of the chat displayed.
Member list pane	See who else is present in the chat room by looking in this pane.
Self-view pane	See what your character looks like after you specify an emotion and before you enter your message.

continues

TABLE 22.1   Continued

Element	Purpose
Emotion wheel	Click one of the faces to change your character's emotion before sending a message.
Compose box	Type the message you wish to pass on here.

Member list pane   Viewing pane   Self-view pane

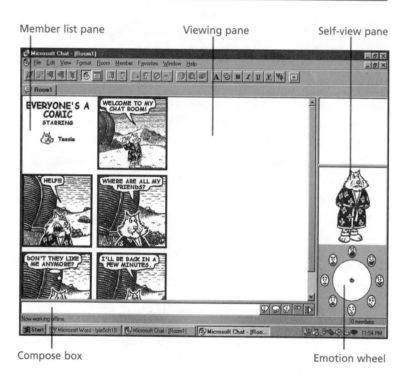

Compose box   Emotion wheel

Figure 22.5 The Microsoft Chat workspace.

Engaging in a Simple Chat

Before we jump head first into the countless buttons on the Microsoft
Chat workspace, I think it will help put things into perspective to outline
chat basics. Typically, you will do the following to engage in a basic chat:

1. Make your way into a chat room of interest as described in previous sections of this lesson.

2. When you're ready to add something, use the emotion wheel to
   make sure the applicable mood is selected.

3. Next, type your message in the compose box.

4. Click Enter to send your message to the group. A comic strip
   panel will appear with your character "saying" the comments
   you typed.

 Talking, thinking, whispering Not only can your character "speak" to the group (click Enter or click the
talk button to the immediate right of the compose
box), you can articulate your thoughts in a thought
bubble as well by clicking the think button to the
right of the talk button. Furthermore, by clicking the
whisper button (to the right of the think button), you
can make a private comment to another member of
the group without the others seeing it. What a great
way to poke fun at another character's bad hair day!

Show, Don't Just Tell

As you've gathered from the mere presence of the emotion wheel,
Microsoft Chat is capable of doing so much more than simply relaying
text and a static picture of your chosen character. You can click a different
face on the emotion wheel on-the-fly to change your character's
expression.

The Chat Toolbar: Your Guide to Advanced Functions at a Glance

Just when you thought we already crammed a lot into this lesson, there's even more. While we can't cover every feature of Microsoft Chat in just one short lesson, we can try to get as far as humanly possible. Believe it or not, the Chat toolbar is an amazingly quick way to access some of the more advanced features of Microsoft Chat without having to plow through scads of menus and dialog boxes.

Table 22.2 gives you a quick look at what each button of the toolbar does. And to make life easier, the buttons are covered from left to right in the order in which they appear on the toolbar.

TABLE 22.2 The Microsoft Chat Toolbar Button Functions

Press This...	...To Do This
	Connect to the chat server.
	Disconnect you from the chat server.
	Enter a chat room.
	Leave a chat room.
	Create a chat room that you'll host.
	Display the chats in Comics view.
	Display the chat in Text view.
	Show a list of people present in the current chat room.
	Open a list of users logged on to the same chat server, no matter what room they're in.

Press This...	...To Do This
	Let others know you've stepped away from your computer.
	Open the user information profile like the one you filled out earlier.
	Keep a certain character's comments from appearing on your display.
	Another way to whisper to another person logged on to the same chat server.
	Send email to the specified character.
	Visit the home page of the specified character.
	Work with a character in NetMeeting.
	Define a new font for use by your character.
	Change the color of a font.
	Make your text bold.
	Make your text italic.
	Underline your text.
	Set your font to fixed pitch.
	Set your text to a symbol font.
	Open your list of favorite documents and Web sites.

In this lesson, you got a quick introduction to Microsoft Chat and its various features. It was a lot of territory to cover, but I'm confident that you'll have enough information to begin playing with the application.

Congratulations, you've completed *Sams Teach Yourself Microsoft Internet Explorer 5 in 10 Minutes*. You should now feel pretty comfortable using Internet Explorer and the other applications contained in the Internet Explorer 5 suite. Even though you've completed all of the lessons, you might find it handy to keep this text nearby to use as a quick reference while you continue to use Internet Explorer 5.

INDEX

A

Accounts command (Tools menu), 144
Active Desktop update, 2-3
Add Favorites dialog box, 59
Address bar, 31
Address Book contact information
    adding, 124-127
        automatically, 127
    composing messages with,
        128-129
    editing, 130-131
Addresses button (Outlook Express
    toolbar), 107
advanced search options (search
    engines), 86
all-in-one pages, 88-89
Altavista Web site, 87
Attach button (Outlook Express),
    111
attaching files to email (Outlook
    Express), 112-113
Attachment column (Outlook
    Express Inbox), 132
attachments (email)
    opening, 136
    reading, 135-137

audio, New Mail Notification sound,
    100-101
Audio Level controls (NetMeeting),
    196
Audio Tuning Wizard, 194
AutoComplete dialog box, saving
    user IDs/passwords, 38
AutoComplete feature, 34
AutoComplete for Forms feature,
    36-37
AutoComplete Settings dialog
    box, 37
automatic email checks (Outlook
    Express), 142
automatic email saves (Outlook
    Express), stopping, 174-175
automatic synchronization (browsing
    offline), 60
AutoSearch feature, 92-93
available disk space, checking, 3-4

B

Back button, 25
Background tab (Chat Connection
    dialog box), 207
bak files (backup files), 3
BCC (blind carbon copy) line, 110
Browse for Folder dialog box, 50

browsing Web sites offline, 59-63
Favorites
    making available offline,
    63-65
    synchronizing, 65-66
    viewing offline, 67-68
synchronization options, 60-64

C

cache, 27
calls (NetMeeting)
    placing, 198
    receiving, 199
canceling posts (newsgroups),
    156-157
Category list (NetMeeting), 196
CC (carbon copy) line, 109
Chat, 6
Chat Connection dialog box,
    204-207
chat servers, 205
    connecting to, 207-209
Chat toolbar (Microsoft Chat),
    212-213
chats
    Microsoft Chat, 203-213
        Chat toolbar buttons,
        212-213
        chats, participating in, 211
        comic strip format,
        203-204
        setting up, 204-209
        Talk button, 211
        Think button, 211
        Whisper button, 211
        workspace, 209-210
    NetMeeting text chat, 200
Check Names button (Outlook
    Express), 111
checking for new email messages
    automatically (Outlook Express),
    142

child protection, 74
    Content Advisor
        disabling, 79
        setting up, 74-78
        settings, changing, 80
    RASC ratings, 74, 77
Clear Forms setting (AutoComplete
    for Forms feature), 37
Clear History option, 38
Clear Passwords option, 39
Close button, 24
comic strip format (Microsoft Chat),
    203-204
commands
    Edit menu, Find, 93
    File menu
        Import and Export, 55-56
        Organize Favorites, 63
        Send Later, 159
    Insert menu
        Hyperlink, 184
        Images, 188
    Tools menu
        Accounts, 144
        Internet Options, 37, 71
        Synchronize, 65, 68
compacting
    mail folders (Outlook Express),
        176
    stored newsgroup messages
        (Outlook Express), 179
Compose Box (Microsoft Chat), 210
Connect tab (Chat Connection dialog
    box), 207
contact information (Outlook
    Express)
    adding to Address Book,
        124-127
        automatically, 127
    composing messages with,
        128-129
    editing, 130-131
Contacts List (Outlook Express), 104

Content Advisor
    disabling, 79
    setting up, 74-78
    settings, changing, 80
Contents tab (help files), 41
cookies, 39
Copy button (Outlook Express), 111
Create Folder dialog box, 165
Create Hyperlink dialog box,
    185-187
cross-posting messages to news-
    groups, 154-155
Current Call window (NetMeeting),
    198
customizing Microsoft Internet Start
    page, 13-18
    Personalize page, 14
Cut button (Outlook Express), 111
C|Net's Search.com Web site, 89

D

Debriefing Web site, 88
default home page, 12
default signatures (Outlook
    Express), setting, 118
defining Message Rules (Outlook
    Express), 168-170
Deja News Web site, 87, 145
Delete button (Outlook Express tool-
    bar), 106
Deleted Items folder (Outlook
    Express), 138
deleting
    email messages (Outlook
        Express), 137-140
        Deleted Items folder, 138
        multiple deletions, 140
        Purge button, 138
        Undelete command, 140
    Favorites (Web sites), 51
    newsgroup messages (Outlook
        Express), 178

desktop shortcuts (Web sites), creat-
    ing, 34, 47-48
dialog boxes
    Add Favorites, 59
    AutoComplete, saving user
        IDs/passwords, 38
    AutoComplete Settings, 37
    Browse for Folder, 50
    Chat Connection, 204-207
    Create Folder, 165
    Create Hyperlink, 185-187
    Enter Network Password, 189
    Favorites, 45
    Find, 93-94
    Find Message, 171
    Image, 188
    Internet Options, 19
    Microsoft Chat Options, 206
    New Page, 185
    Organize Favorites, 49, 63
    Rule Editor, 168
    Select Recipients, 128-129
    Sounds Properties, 101
    Spelling, 122-123
DigiSearch Web site, 88
Directory Listing (NetMeeting),
    196-197
disabling Content Advisor, 79
Dogpile Web site, 88
domain names, 107
downloading
    Internet Explorer 5, 4-5
        troubleshooting, 11
    newsgroup messages (offline
        browsing), 162-164

E

Edit menu commands, 24
    Find, 93
editing contact information (Outlook
    Express), 130-131
email, *see* Outlook Express
email servers, adding to Outlook
    Express, 95-98

Emotion Wheel (Microsoft Chat), 210-211
Enter Network Password dialog box, 189
Excite Web site, 84, 86
exporting Favorites lists, 55-56

F

Favorites (Web sites), 43
    deleting, 51
    desktop shortcuts, creating, 47-48
    exporting Favorites lists, 55-56
        via email, 57
    importing Favorites lists, 56-57
        via email, 57
    links, emailing, 52-53
    making available offline, 63-66
        synchronization, 65-66
    organizing in folders, 49-50
    pages, emailing, 53-54
    saving, 44-45
    selecting, 43-44
    sharing, 52
    viewing, 46-47
        offline, 67-68
Favorites button, 28-29
Favorites dialog box, 45
file attachments (email)
    adding to messages, 112-113
    opening, 136
    reading, 135-137
File menu commands, 24
    Import and Export, 55-56
    Organize Favorites, 63
    Send Later, 159
files
    bak files (backup files), 3
    help files
        Contents tab, 41
        Index tab, 41
        Search tab, 41
        searching, 40-42

signature files (Outlook Express)
    applying to outgoing messages, 121
    creating, 116-118
    default signatures, setting, 118
    telling Outlook which to use, 119-120
    tmp files (temporary files), 3
filtering email (Outlook Express), 167-170
Find command (Edit menu), 93
Find dialog box, 93-94
Find Message dialog box, 171
Find Message window (Outlook Express), 172
finding
    newsgroups, 145-148
        Deja News Web site, 145
        messages (Outlook Express), 170-172
    Web sites, 81-82
        AutoSearch feature, 92-93
        Search Assistant, 90-91
        search engines, 85-89
        specified page searches, 93-94
        subject indexes, 83-85
Flag column (Outlook Express Inbox), 132
flame wars, 146
Folder Bar (Outlook Express), 104
Folder List (Outlook Express), 104
folders
    compacting mail folders (Outlook Express), 176
    Deleted Items folder (Outlook Express), 138
    Favorites (Web sites), organizing, 49-50
    saving email messages (Outlook Express), 165-166
    Sent Items Folder (Outlook Express), 174

Formatting toolbar (Outlook Express), 112
formatting Web page text, 182-184
forms, AutoComplete for Forms feature, 36-37
Forward button, 25
Forward Message button (Outlook Express toolbar), 106
forwarding
    email messages (Outlook Express), 141
    newsgroup messages, 153
From column (Outlook Express Inbox), 132
FrontPage Express, 6
    Web pages
        formatting text, 182-184
        images, adding, 188
        links, creating, 184-187
        publishing, 189-190
    workspace, 181
FTP servers, saving Web pages to, 189-190
fullscreen mode, 32

G-H

Go menu, 25

hard disk, checking available space, 3-4
headers (newsgroups), downloading, 162-164
help files, 41
    searching, 40-42
Help menu, 25
History button, 29-30
Home button, 27
HotBot Web site, 86
Hyperlink command (Insert menu), 184

I-J-K

icons
    Inbox icon (Outlook Express), 99
    Internet Explorer icon, 32
    Outlook Express icon, 95
Image dialog box, 188
imagemaps, 33
images, adding to Web pages, 188
Images command (Insert menu), 188
IMAP (Internet Message Access Protocol), 97
IMAP servers, 134
Import and Export command (File menu), 55-56
Import/Export Wizard, 55-57
importing
    email messages into Outlook Express, 99-100
    Favorites lists, 56-57
Inbox (Outlook Express), 104, 132-133
Inbox icon (Outlook Express), 99
Index tab (help files), 41
Infoseek Web site, 84, 87
Insert menu commands
    Hyperlink, 184
    Images, 188
installing
    Internet Explorer 5, 2-4
        components, 5-7
        download process, 4-5
        free disk space, checking, 3-4
        Setup Wizard, 5-10
        troubleshooting, 11
    Windows Active Desktop update, 2-3
Internet Accounts window (Outlook Express), 95
Internet Connection Wizard, 96-98

Internet Explorer 5
    components, 5-7
        FrontPage Express, 6
        Microsoft Chat, 6
        Microsoft Wallet, 7
        NetMeeting, 6
        Outlook Express, 6
    installing, 2-4
        components, 5-7
        download process, 4-5
        free disk space, checking,
            3-4
        Setup Wizard, 5-10
        troubleshooting, 11
        Windows Active Desktop
            update, 2-3
    obtaining, 1-2
    screen elements, 21-32
        Address bar, 31
        Back button, 25
        Close button, 24
        Edit menu, 24
        Favorites button, 28-29
        File menu, 24
        Forward button, 25
        Go menu, 25
        Help menu, 25
        History button, 29-30
        Home button, 27
        Internet Explorer icon, 32
        Mail button, 31
        Maximize/Restore
            button, 23
        Minimize button, 23
        Print button, 31
        Refresh button, 26
        scrollbars, 32
        Search button, 27
        Stop button, 26
        title bar, 21
        View menu, 24
    updating, 11
Internet Explorer icon, 32
Internet Message Access Protocol
    (IMAP), 97

Internet Options command (Tools
    menu), 37, 71
Internet Options dialog box, 19
Internet security, 69
    Content Advisor
        disabling, 79
        setting up, 74-78
        settings, changing, 80
    security zones, 69-70
        assigning Web sites to,
            72-74
        Internet Zone, 70
        levels of security,
            setting, 71
        Local Intranet Zone, 70
        removing Web sites
            from, 74
        Restricted Sites Zone, 70
        Trusted Sites Zone, 70
Internet Sleuth Web site, 89
Internet Start page, 12-13, 18-20
    default Start page, 12
    defining new Start pages, 19-20
    Microsoft Internet Start
        page, 12
        customizing, 13-18
Internet Zone (security zone), 70

L

levels of security (security zones),
    setting, 71
links, 33
    emailing Favorite Web site
        links, 52-53
    imagemaps, 33
links (Web pages)
    creating, 184-187
        between sites, 186-187
        within same site, 184-186
Local Intranet Zone (security
    zone), 70
Lycos Web site, 84, 87

M

Mail button, 31
Mail/News Column Headers
(Outlook Express), 105
Mark for Retrieval column (Outlook
Express Inbox), 132
marking newsgroup messages as
read (Outlook Express), 176-178
Maximize/Restore button, 23
Member List pane (Microsoft Chat),
209
menu bar, 24-25
Message List box (Outlook
Express), 132-133
Message Rules (Outlook Express),
167-170
defining, 168-170
Message toolbar (Outlook Express),
110-112
meta-search engines, 87-88
Microsoft Chat, 6, 203-213
Chat toolbar buttons, 212-213
chats, participating in, 211
comic strip format, 203-204
setting up, 204-209
backgrounds, selecting,
207
chat identities, establish-
ing, 206-207
chat servers, connecting
to, 207-209
personal information, pro-
viding, 204-206
Talk button, 211
Think button, 211
Whisper button, 211
workspace, 209-210
Microsoft Chat Options dialog box,
206
Microsoft Internet Start page, 12
customizing, 13-18
Personalize page, 14
Microsoft Search Assistant, 27
Microsoft Wallet, 7

Microsoft Web site
downloading Internet Explorer 5,
4-5
updating Internet Explorer 5, 11
migrating, 98
Minimize button, 23
Mining Company Web site, 84

N

Nerdworld Web site, 84
NetMeeting, 6, 191-192
Current Call window, 198
placing calls, 198
receiving calls, 199
setting up, 192-195
text chat, 200
whiteboard, 201
workspace, 195-197
NetMeeting Setup Wizard, 192
New Mail Notification sound
(Outlook Express), changing,
100-101
New Message button (Outlook
Express toolbar), 106
New Message Dropdown Arrow
(Outlook Express toolbar), 106
New Message window (Outlook
Express), 107
New Page dialog box, 185
news servers, adding to Outlook
Express, 144-145
newsgroups
finding, 145-148
Deja News Web site, 145
flame wars, 146
messages
compacting stored mes-
sages (Outlook Express),
179
deleting (Outlook Express),
178
finding (Outlook Express),
170-172

forwarding, 153
marking as read (Outlook Express), 176-178
posting, 154-157
printing, 152
replies, viewing, 158
replying to, 153
saving, 152
viewing only new messages (Outlook Express), 176-178
reading, 150-154
downloading specific messages, 162-164
offline, 160-164
plus signs, 151
threads, 151
spam, 145
subscribing to, 148
synchronization, 161-162
unsubscribing to, 149

O

offline browsing, 59-63
email messages, composing, 159-160
Favorites, 63-65
synchronizing, 65-66
viewing, 67-68
newsgroups
downloading specific messages, 162-164
reading, 160-164
synchronization, 161-162
synchronization options, 60-64
Offline Favorite Wizard, 60-64
Open Attachment Warning box (Outlook Express), 136
opening file attachments (email), 136
Organize Favorites commands (File menu), 63
Organize Favorites dialog box, 49, 63

Outlook Express, 6, 95
Address Book
adding contact information, 124-127
composing messages with, 128-129
editing contact information, 130-131
automatic email checks, 142
BCC (blind carbon copy) line, 110
CC (carbon copy) line, 109
compacting mail folders, 176
email messages
attaching files to, 112-113
automatic email saves, stopping, 174-175
composing, 107-112
composing offline, 159-160
deleting, 137-140
file attachments, reading, 135-137
folders, creating, 165
forwarding, 141
importing into Outlook, 99-100
message body, creating, 110-112
reading, 134-135
replying to, 141
saving, 141
sending to multiple recipients, 109-110
sending to one recipient, 107-108
email servers, adding, 95-98
emailing Web sites
links, 52-53
pages, 53-54
Find Message window, 172
IMAP server support, 134
Import Wizard, 99-100
Inbox icon, 99
Internet Accounts window, 95
Message List box, 132-133

Message Rules, 167-170
  defining, 168-170
migrating to, 98
New Mail Notification sound,
  changing, 100-101
New Message window, 107
news servers, adding, 144-145
newsgroup messages
  canceling posts, 156-157
  compacting stored mes-
    sages, 179
  cross-posting messages,
    154-155
  deleting, 178
  finding, 145-148, 170-172
  flame wars, 146
  forwarding, 153
  marking as read, 176-178
  plus signs, 151
  posting, 154-156
  printing, 152
  reading, 150-154
  reading offline, 160-164
  replying to, 153
  saving, 152
  spam, 145, 155
  subscribing to, 148
  synchronization, 161-162
  threads, 151
  unsubscribing to, 149
  viewing only new mes-
    sages, 176-178
  viewing replies to posted
    messages, 158
Preview pane, 134
screen elements, 103-107
  Formatting toolbar, 112
  Message toolbar, 110-112
  toolbar, 105-107
Sent Items folder, 174
signatures
  applying to outgoing mes-
    sages, 121
  creating, 116-118
  default signatures, setting,
    118

  telling Outlook which to
    use, 119-120
  spell checker, 121-123
  stationery, 114-116
Outlook Express icon, 95

P-Q

padlock symbol, 73
pages (Web sites), emailing, 53-54
paper clip button (Outlook Express),
  112
passwords, saving, 38
Paste button (Outlook Express), 111
Personal Info tab (Chat Connection
  dialog box), 205
Personalize page (Internet Start
  page), 14-18
plus signs (newgroups), 151
posting messages to newsgroups,
  154-157
  canceling posts, 156-157
  crossposting, 154, 155
  spamming, 155
  viewing replies, 158
Preview pane (Outlook Express), 134
Print button, 31
  Outlook Express toolbar, 106
printing newsgroup messages, 152
Priority column (Outlook Express
  Inbox), 132
publishing Web pages, 189-190
Purge button (Outlook Express), 138

R

reading
  email messages (Outlook
    Express), 134-135
    file attachments, 135-137
  newsgroups, 150-154
    downloading specific mes-
      sages, 162-164

offline, 160-164
plus signs, 151
synchronization, 161-162
threads, 151
Received column (Outlook Express Inbox), 133
Refresh button, 26
Reply to All button (Outlook Express toolbar), 106
Reply to Author button (Outlook Express toolbar), 106
replying to
  email messages (Outlook Express), 141
  newsgroup messages, 153
Restricted Sites Zone (security zone), 70
RSAC (Recreational Software Advisory Council) ratings, 74, 77
Rule Editor dialog box, 168
running Setup Wizard, 5

S

saving
  email messages (Outlook Express), 141
    automatic saves, stopping, 174-175
    folders, creating, 165-166
  newsgroup messages, 152
  passwords, 38
  user IDs, 38
  Web pages to FTP servers, 189-190
  Web sites as Favorites, 44-45
screen elements
  Internet Explorer 5, 21-32
    Address bar, 31
    Back button, 25
    Close button, 24
    Edit menu, 24
    Favorites button, 28-29
    File menu, 24

Forward button, 25
Go menu, 25
Help menu, 25
History button, 29-30
Home button, 27
Internet Explorer icon, 32
Mail button, 31
Maximize/Restore button, 23
Minimize button, 23
Print button, 31
Refresh button, 26
scrollbars, 32
Search button, 27
Stop button, 26
title bar, 21
View menu, 24
  Outlook Express, 103-107
    Formatting toolbar, 112
    Message toolbar, 110-112
    toolbar, 105-107
scrollbars, 32
Search Assistant, 27, 90-91
Search button, 27
search engines, 85-89
  advanced search options, 86
  all-in-one pages, 88-89
    C\Net's Search.com, 89
    Internet Sleuth, 89
  Altavista, 87
  DejaNews, 87
  Excite, 86
  HotBot, 86
  Infoseek, 87
  Lycos, 87
  meta-search engines, 87-88
Search tab (help files), 41
searching
  help files, 40-42
  newsgroups, 145-148
    Deja News Web site, 145
    messages, 170-172
  Web sites, 81-82
    AutoSearch feature, 92-93
    Search Assistant, 90-91

search engines, 85-89
specified pages, 93-94
subject indexes, 83-85
secure servers, 73
security, 69
    Content Advisor
        disabling, 79
        setting up, 74-78
        settings, changing, 80
    security zones, 69-70
        assigning Web sites to,
            72-74
        Internet Zone, 70
        levels of security,
            setting, 71
        Local Intranet Zone, 70
        removing Web sites
            from, 74
        Restricted Sites Zone, 70
        Trusted Sites Zone, 70
Select Recipients dialog box,
    128-129
Self-View pane (Microsoft Chat),
    209
Send and Receive button (Outlook
    Express toolbar), 106
Send button (Outlook Express), 111
Send Later command (File menu),
    159
sending email messages
    to multiple recipients, 109-110
    to one recipient, 107-108
Sent Items folder (Outlook Express),
    174
Server list (NetMeeting), 196
servers
    chat servers, 205
        connecting to, 207-209
    email servers, adding to
        Outlook Express, 95-98
    IMAP servers, 134
Set Priority button (Outlook
    Express), 111

Set Priority Drop-down Arrow
    (Outlook Express), 112
setting up NetMeeting, 192-195
settings
    AutoComplete for Forms fea-
        ture, 37
    Content Advisor, changing, 80
Setup Wizard, 7-10
    running, 5
sharing Favorite Web sites, 52
shortcuts (to Web sites), creating, 34
    Favorites, 47-48
signatures (Outlook Express)
    applying to outgoing messages,
        121
    creating, 116-118
    default signatures, setting, 118
    telling Outlook which to use,
        119-120
sounds, New Mail Notification sound
    (Outlook Express), 100-101
Sounds Properties dialog box, 101
spam, 145, 155
    filtering (Outlook Express), 167
spell checker (Outlook Express),
    121-123
Spelling button (Outlook Express),
    111
Spelling dialog box, 122-123
Start pages, 12-20
    default, 12
    defining, 19-20
    Microsoft Internet Start
        page, 12
        customizing, 13-18
stationery (Outlook Express),
    114-116
Status Bar (Outlook Express), 105
Stop button, 26
Subject column (Outlook Express
    Inbox), 133
subject indexes, 83-85
subscribing to newsgroups, 148

synchronization (browsing offline),
    60-64
    Favorite Web sites, 65-66
    newsgroup synchronization,
        161-162
Synchronize command (Tools
    menu), 65, 68

T

Talk button (Microsoft Chat), 211
text (Web page text), formatting,
    182-184
text chat (NetMeeting), 200
Think button (Microsoft Chat), 211
threads (newgroups), 151
title bar, 21
tmp files (temporary files), 3
toolbars
    Chat toolbar (Microsoft Chat),
        212-213
    Formatting toolbar (Outlook
        Express), 112
    Message toolbar (Outlook
        Express), 110-112
    Outlook Express toolbar,
        105-107
Tools menu commands
    Accounts, 144
    Internet Options, 37, 71
    Synchronize, 65, 68
troubleshooting Internet Explorer 5
    installation, 11
Trusted Sites Zone (security
    zone), 70

U

Undelete command (Outlook
    Express), 140
Undo button (Outlook Express), 111
unsubscribing to newsgroups, 149
updating Internet Explorer 5, 11
user IDs, saving, 38

V

View menu, 24
viewing
    Favorite Web sites, 46-47
        offline, 67-68
    newsgroup messages (Outlook
        Express), 176-178
        replies, 158
Viewing pane (Microsoft Chat), 209

W

Wallet, 7
Web pages
    creating
        formatting text, 182-184
        images, adding, 188
        links, 184-187
    publishing, 189-190
Web Publishing Wizard, 189-190
Web sites
    accessing, 33-35
        imagemaps, 33
        links, 33
    Altavista, 87
    browsing offline, 59-63
        synchronization options,
            60-64
    CINet's Search.com, 89
    Debriefing, 88
    Deja News, 87, 145
    desktop shortcuts, creating, 34
    DigiSearch, 88
    Dogpile, 88
    Excite, 84, 86
    Favorites, 43
        deleting, 51
        desktop shortcuts, creating,
            47-48
        exporting Favorites lists,
            55-57
        importing Favorites lists,
            56-57

links, emailing, 52-53
making available offline,
    63-65
organizing in folders,
    49-50
pages, emailing, 53-54
saving, 44-45
selecting, 43-44
sharing, 52
synchronizing (browsing
    offline), 65-66
viewing, 46-47
viewing offline, 67-68
HotBot, 86
Infoseek, 84, 87
Internet Sleuth, 89
Lycos, 84, 87
Microsoft
    downloading Internet
        Explorer 5, 4-5
    updating Internet
        Explorer 5, 11
Mining Company, 84
Nerdworld, 84
RSAC ratings, 74, 77
searching, 81-82
    AutoSearch feature, 92-93
    Search Assistant, 90-91
    search engines, 85-89
    specified pages, 93-94
    subject indexes, 83-85
security zones
    assigning, 72-74
    removing, 74
Yahoo!, 83-85
Whisper button (Microsoft Chat),
    211
whiteboard (NetMeeting), 201
Windows Active Desktop update,
    2-3
wizards
    Audio Tuning Wizard, 194
    Import/Export Wizard, 55-57
    Internet Connection Wizard,
        96-98

NetMeeting Setup Wizard, 192
Offline Favorite Wizard, 60-64
Outlook Express Import Wizard,
    99-100
Setup Wizard, 7-10
    running, 5
Web Publishing Wizard,
    189-190
workspaces
    FrontPage Express, 181
    Microsoft Chat, 209-210
    NetMeeting, 195-197

X-Y-Z

Yahoo! Web site, 83-85

zones (security zones), 69-70
    assigning Web sites to, 72-74
    Internet Zone, 70
    levels of security, setting, 71
    Local Intranet Zone, 70
    removing Web sites from, 74
    Restricted Sites Zone, 70
    Trusted Sites Zone, 70

SAMS
Teach Yourself
in 10 Minutes

Quick steps for fast results™

Sams Teach Yourself in 10 Minutes *gets you the results you want—fast! Work through the 10-minute lessons and learn everything you need to know quickly and easily. It's the handiest resource for the information you're looking for.*

Sams Teach Yourself the Internet in 10 Minutes, Second Edition

Galen Grimes
0-672-31610-2
$12.99 US/$21.95 CAN

Other Sams Teach Yourself in 10 Minutes Titles

Microsoft Office 2000
Laura Acklen
0-672-31431-2
$12.99 US/$21.95 CAN

Microsoft FrontPage 2000
Galen Grimes
0-672-31498-3
$12.99 US/$21.95 CAN

Microsoft Outlook 2000
Joe Habraken
0-672-31450-9
$12.99 US/$21.95 CAN

Microsoft Word 2000
Peter Aitken
0-672-31441-x
$12.99 US/$21.95 CAN

Microsoft Excel 2000
Jennifer Fulton
0-672-31457-6
$12.99 US/$21.95 CAN

Microsoft PowerPoint 2000
Faithe Wempen
0-672-31440-1
$12.99 US/$21.95 CAN

Microsoft Access 2000
Faithe Wempen
0-672-31487-8
$12.99 US/$21.95 CAN

Microsoft Publisher 2000
Joe Habraken
0-672-31569-6
$12.99 US/$21.95 CAN

Windows 98
Jennifer Fulton
0-672-31330-8
$12.99 US/$21.95 CAN

All prices are subject to change.

SAMS

www.samspublishing.com